WOOL-GATHERING.

BY

GAIL HAMILTON,

AUTHOR OF "COUNTRY LIVING AND COUNTRY THINKING," "GALA-DAYS," ETC.

BOSTON:
TICKNOR AND FIELDS.
1867.

UNIVERSITY PRESS: WELCH, BIGELOW, & CO.,
CAMBRIDGE.

CONTENTS.

CHAPTER I.

CHAPTER II.

CHAPTER III.

CHAPTER IV.

CHAPTER V.

CHAPTER VI.

CHAPTER VII.

CHAPTER VIII.

CHAPTER IX.

CHAPTER X.

CHAPTER XI.

WOOL-GATHERING.

CHAPTER I.

Raison d'être. — The Commissariat. — A bad Beginning. — Goths and Vandals. — Moral Reflections. — Natural History of Niagara. — The Badness of Women. — Moral Reflections. — The Goodness of Men. — More Moral Reflections. — Tact against Temper. — A Negation of Moral Reflections. — A Baby. — Two Babies. — Eloquent Outburst on Chicago. — Chicago itself. — Unhappy Girl in Chicago. — Inexperienced happy Pair in Chicago Station. — Experienced happy Quartette in Chicago Station. — Predisposing Causes of the happy Pair. — Happy Family in Chicago Station. — Distressed Woman in Chicago Station. — Wisconsin. — Distressed Woman continued. — Distressed Woman concluded.

ABOUT a year ago I came into possession of a fortune. It was from an entirely unexpected source, and I naturally cast about for the best mode of investment. The war was bravely over, and there was no further need of private contributions to prop up public credit. Diligent investigation showed that wool-growing was a delightful and profitable occupation.

Sheep are innocent, lambs engaging, and wool marketable. I therefore despatched my agent to Wisconsin, where he bought twenty-five sheep, at four dollars and fifty cents a head. This amounted to one hundred and twelve dollars and fifty cents. I gave him the odd half-dollar for commission, bade him put the remaining twelve dollars (I forgot to mention that the original fortune was one hundred and twenty-five dollars) into the bank against a rainy day, drive the sheep to Minnesota, and set them spinning, — by metonymy. He wrote to me soon that he had faithfully carried out all my directions; the sheep had been bought and driven home, and were in good condition. He added, however, that there was always a degree of uncertainty connected with the establishing of a family of sheep. A greater or less number generally succumbed to the severity of their first winter in a new climate. I wrote back at once that I did not expect the order of nature to be changed for my benefit, but neither did I wish to be annoyed by dead sheep dribbling through the winter. It could not be exhilarating to read, in every letter that came, "there is another sheep frozen." I therefore bade him not write any obituary notices, but wait till the sheep were all dead, and then say so.

I accordingly heard no bad news from my sheep. And some time during the following summer word came that the sheep-shearing was over, and my agent was ready with his first yearly report. It was a beautiful document. It showed that my profits were two pounds of wool to each sheep. This my agent had sold for forty-five cents a pound, making ninety cents a head, which, multiplied by twenty-five heads, made twenty-two dollars and fifty cents as a year's interest of one hundred and twelve dollars and fifty cents. I have verified this reckoning by geometry and the higher mathematics, and I believe it to be correct in every particular.

The thoughtful reader will not fail to see that twenty-two dollars and fifty cents is a sum of money not to be laughed at, and the question at once became, how to get possession of it. The United States Post-Office does not refund the property which it fails to transmit, and, considering the heavy robberies committed upon the Adams Express Company, I could not trust my treasure to its keeping. After a severe mental conflict I decided to go myself and fetch the money. Commentators differ as to the real motive of my journey, but this is the explanation on which the general opinion of foreign nations and the next age will finally settle.

Aware that mankind is ever athirst for knowledge, I have decided to gratify it by putting on record some of the more sagacious thoughts which naturally occur to the inquiring mind on its tour round the world. I shall not descend to the trivial details of personal experience, which are necessarily impertinent, but shall adhere strictly to such broad and philosophic views as have a national, I may say a cosmopolitan value. And I shall from time to time add moral reflections; two reasons impel me to this: mankind is fond of reading moral reflections; and I am fond of making them.

The first requisite for a long journey is to take all your best clothes. A prejudice prevails to some extent against this practice, and it is indeed unwise if you regard clothes solely as a means of warmth; but the noble soul lifts its wardrobe into a higher sphere, and makes it an element of character. You may in truth not need to array your self in all your glory, but the consciousness that you can do it gives a peace of mind which outweighs many trunks.

Next in importance to your best clothes are two bottles of Dr. Hamlin's cholera mixture. When I say that Dr. Hamlin is an Orthodox Congregational clergyman, I need give no further reason for my recommendation; but I can from my own knowledge speak with confidence of the efficacy of his medicine. For nine weeks it travelled with us by field and flood, and not one of the party had the cholera!

A bottle of brandy makes an excellent travelling-companion if your principles and habits are good.

A box of mustard is an ounce of prevention. If your eye-teeth are as yet at an immature stage of development, you will order five bottles of potted tongue, beef, and herring, — small stone jars, each one holding, judging from your experience of meats, enough to last through two lunches. Opening them, you find them packed with salted fire, of which you can endure a morsel only by spreading it on a cracker with the tip of your fruit-knife to the last degree of imperceptibility. If any person is designing to provision a fleet for Arctic explorations, let him apply to the publishers of this book before purchasing elsewhere, and he will hear of something very much to his advantage.

Beguiled by pleasant memories, you will order also three dozen spiced and pickled lambs' tongues; and believe me, gentle reader, you have no conception till you see them together, how many tongues thirty-six spiced and pickled lambs have! When you reflect that these are to be carried about with you till they are eaten, you see that lambs are not the only innocents which are in a pickle, and the situation becomes appalling. But I forbear.

Let us suppose now that your various viands are snugly bestowed, and yourself fairly started on your journey. The first thing you know, your basket bounces off the car-seat, and rolls over and over down the aisle. There is a rattling of crockery, and a sudden suspicion that your whole basket has turned into a cholera mixture. You are too much ashamed to take account of stock in public, but now and then put your nose down furtively to the crack of the lid to ascertain what smell seems to be uppermost, and are relieved at the absence of any prevailing perfume. By the time your series of observations are conducted to a satisfactory conclusion you are in Albany, the capital of the State of New York, the seat of a Legislature remarkable in an age of general uprightness for the purity of its morals and the incorruptibility of its legislation.

Here we stop for the night. The best house in Albany is said to be the Vandal House. You are shown into a room that has not been opened since its occupant left it, and is unsavory and untidy to the last degree. An appeal to the gentlemanly clerk secures a change for the better; but there is a hole by the fireplace in Number Two that looks suspicious. You cross-examine the porter, who assures you that it has no significance whatever. A mouse in that room is an event of which history gives no record. Nevertheless, you take the precaution to stuff the hole with an old *New York Herald*, and are awakened at midnight by the dreadful rustling of paper. A dreadful gnawing succeeds the dreadful rustling, and away goes a boot in the direction of the sound. There is a pause broken only by heart throbs! Then another gnawing, followed by a boot till the supply is exhausted. Then you begin on the pillows. A longer pause gives rise to the hope that order is about to reign in Warsaw, and you are just falling asleep again, when a smart scratching close to your ear, shoots you to the other side of the room with the conviction that the mouse is running up the folds of the curtain at the head of your bed. In a frenzy you ring violently, and ask through the door for a chambermaid.

"Can't have no chambermaid this time o' night," drawls the porter sleepily.

"Then send up a mouse-trap."

"Aint no mouse-trap in the house."

"Then bring a cat!"

"Dunno nothin' about it," and he scuffs his slippered feet down the long gallery, growling audibly, poor fellow, half suspecting evidently that he is the victim of a joke; but alas! it is no joke.

You mount sentry on the foot of the bed, facing the enemy. He emerges from the curtain, runs up and down the slats of the blind in innocent glee, flaunts across the window-seat, flashing every now and then into obscurity; and this is the worst of all. When you see him he is in one place, but when you do not see him he is everywhere. You hold fast your umbrella, and from time to time make vigorous raps on the floor to keep him out of your immediate vicinity, and so the night wears wearily away. Your refreshing sleep turns into a campaign against a mouse, for which agreeable entertainment you pay in the morning three dollars and a half; and the gentlemanly clerk, with a pitying smile, informs you, "O, we cannot help that! There are mice all over the house!"

Moral reflection: If ever the education of a soaring human boy be intrusted to my care, I will endeavor to model his manners on those of a clerk in a hotel. For conscious superiority, tempered with benevolence and swathed in suavity; for perfect self-possession; for high-bred condescension to the ignorance and toleration of the weakness of others; for absolute equality to circumstances, and a certain grace, assurance, and flourish of bearing, — give me a clerk in a hotel. We may see generals, poets, and philosophers, indistinguishable from the common herd; but a true hotel clerk wears on his beauteous brow, and in his noble mien, the indubitable sign of greatness.

From Albany to Niagara is a pleasant day's journey, and the Niagara mice are not quite so large, nor quite so lively, as those of Eastern New York. They do not appear till the second day. Then, resting quietly after a walk, you see a mouse creep timidly from under the bureau. You improvise a sort of pontoon bridge to the bell, out of your chairs and tables, and, as it is day-time, secure a chambermaid and superintend a mouse-hunt. She whisks about the room enthusiastically, peers under all the furniture, assuring you the while that it is four years now she has been in the house and never saw a mouse in the chambers, though she confesses to having seen them in the kitchen, and, being hard pressed, well, she *has* seen them in the passages; but in the chambers, no! never! and you are led to believe that, though a mouse might stand shivering on the brink of your room, he would fear to step foot over the threshold. No, there is no mouse here, not a sign of a mouse.

"No sign of a mouse, except the mouse itself," you suggest.

"Ah! but you must have been mistaken. It was a shadow. Why," (with a grand flourish of the valance with her right hand, and in the air with her left,) "you can see for yourself there is no mouse here," — and she thinks she has made her point.

You look at her, debating within yourself whether it is worth while to attempt to acquaint her with the true province of negatives, the proper disposition of the burden of proof, and the sophistry of an undue assumption of the major premise, and decide that it is not.

Moral and philological reflection: We see now the reason why trunks and travelling-bags are called traps. Synecdoche: Because the mouse-traps are the most important part of your luggage.

There is said to be a very fine waterfall at Niagara, but I do not know much about it. I remember that I did hear a sort of rushing and roaring under the window.

I will now tell you a story. At Erie, a decently dressed young woman, with a pale, fragile-looking little girl entered the car, and attempted to go past a gentleman to an inside seat. He told her that seat was occupied by a person who had just stepped out. She pushed against him, still determined to enter, and he had to put up his arm to keep her out, but only resisting, not pushing her. Some one then told her that it was the gentleman's wife who occupied the seat. "O, if it was a lady, she begged pardon! She did not know it was a lady," and went a few steps away to take an outside seat by a young girl. The latter told her that also was engaged. "Engaged!" in a loud voice. "Who engaged it? How much did he pay for it extra?" And she flounced into it in a state of high indignation. After the cars started, the occupant of the seat came in, looked at her doubtfully, and then spoke. Her reply was not audible to the other passengers, but it evidently startled him. He glanced around upon the others, half questioning, half smiling, whispered to his young companion, and retreated, taking his stand by the door. The woman then began to laugh, in a loud, boisterous manner, and a gentleman behind her beckoned to the one whose seat she had taken, and, after consultation, removed the girl from her unpleasant proximity to the woman, and gave her his own seat. They then tried to induce the little girl to sit with her mother, but she, poor child, refused, and no one could find it in his heart to force her. Thus, by her evil behavior, the woman had dispossessed of their seats two men and one woman, and had secured three seats for herself. When the conductor came in she gave him a ticket to Buffalo, although she was on a Cleveland train. He told her she was on the wrong train, must get out at the next station, and wait for a Buffalo train. No, she had changed her mind, and was going back to Cleveland. Then she must pay the fare. But the fare was just what she refused to pay, proffering only her Buffalo ticket. The brakeman was ordered in at the next station, and told to take her out. She was so strong and so spirited, both literally and figuratively, that he could not do it, and the conductor had to take hold; between them both they hustled her out, the little girl crying and clinging to her, and calling, "O mamma! mamma!" Fairly off the train, and seeing herself reduced to the necessity of paying or staying, she consented to pay, and entered the car again. At a small station a little farther on she changed her mind once more, and got out. The last seen of her, as the train moved on, she was brandishing her fist, and shouting, "I 've got fifty dollars in my pocket, — yes, a hundred, —

and I'll bet the whole of it I'll have that conductor licked, the minute I get to Cleveland!"

Can anything be more sad than this? Yet the scene was not without its pleasant features. There was much good, honorable, manly feeling shown, much sympathy by those who only saw the expulsion, and not its causes. In a world where women suffer so much without pity, it is a vexatious thing to see pity lavished upon a woman who does not deserve it; but it is good to know that the warm heart is there. A party of drovers, I should think, men rough of beard and gruff of voice, shook their heads. They "hated to see a man lay hands on a woman." They "never wanted to see a woman shoved about that way, no matter what she did." A crowd was continually gathering about her; a crowd closed in around the scuffle; a crowd listened to her haranguing on the platform; but the only violent words I heard were those which came from her own lips. There was every disposition to give the woman her own way, simply because she was a woman, yet there was no disposition to interfere with the legal right of the conductor. Some, who thought the woman was put out for having taken the wrong train, maintained earnestly that the conductor was in the wrong. She had a right to change her mind. No matter if she did buy her ticket in the morning for Buffalo; if she wanted now to go back to Cleveland she had a right to go, and the conductor had no right to stop her.

Moral reflections: So doubly a pity is it when a woman misbehaves, pity for the wrong she does to herself, but pity a thousand times more for the wrong thus put upon those to whom she should be the embodiment of beneficence. The deference which men show to women is no mere chance, civility, custom, or compliment, however they intend it. It is instinctive, and it shows where a woman has vantage-ground to work upon humanity. When she fails to meet this outcoming reverence with a corresponding worthiness, her failure is man's loss. Gentle or vulgar, his soul is wounded in its most delicate susceptibilities, although he may not know it. The harsh blow blunts his sensibility to the soft touch. What cruel training had wrought a coarse, violent woman from a tender little girl I do not know, but I do know that the cruel training had builded worse than it knew. Beyond all its consequences as an intelligent act, every woman's fault is every man's misfortune.

Let me tell you another story. We are in no hurry to reach our journey's end, and if you were not reading this, the chances are you would be doing something worse.

A pleasant hotel piazza, never mind where. A sunny Indian-summer evening. Guests sitting about in careless conversation. Children playing in the yard below. A woman, the most striking of all the company, not exactly beautiful, but with a certain comeliness, an elegance of dress and demeanor, that give a far stronger sense of beauty than does beauty without them. She is sitting with that attractiveness in repose that bespeaks grace in motion, her wise, white fingers gleaming and glancing in the silken meshes of some fine, feminine work. A young man drives bravely by with a young woman at his side. A little boy, the son of the beautiful woman, — on the whole, she *is* beautiful, — with a boy's carelessness, lets fly his arrow straight at one of the high-spirited horses. He prances and curvets up the street, and the mother chides her boy for his heedless act. The young man, as soon as he can curb his startled horses, whirls them about, drives back furiously to the hotel, reins them in suddenly, and with flashing eyes and angry color begins, — " I should think some of you gentlemen," — but he never tells his thought. Sweeps down upon him a vision of grace and grandeur; for the mother had seen him as he turned, divined the

> " Thunder gathering on his brow,
> Lightning flashing from his eye,"

flung aside the light entanglements of her hands, rose quickly as a goddess might have risen, glided — no, swept — I have used the word before, but I know no other to express the dignity of her movement — swept down the path, and flooded and drowned his angry questioning with her full, clear, melodious voice, " Will you permit me, Sir, to apologize ? " The change in the young man's feelings and demeanor was so sudden and complete, as to be almost ludicrous. He had, as he supposed, run full tilt against some evil-minded men, and found instead a beautiful woman at his feet. He had waged war, and peace smothered him with flowers. His coat of mail melted off from him and left him defenceless. He could hardly permit her to tell her story. He blushed, he hesitated, he apologized! and I rather think he rode away with a vague conviction that he had shot a fine woman.

There is no moral to this story. I told it because it is so pretty a picture in my memory that I like to unfold it.

All this time we have been rushing on through the interminable wild rain, and the interminable tame prairies, broad levels of marsh and field, — Ohio, Indiana, Illinois, — fertile and fair in the sunshine perhaps, but inexpressibly dismal and water-soaked now. And here is a little Western baby, who puts us all to shame with his philosophy. A handsome little fellow is he, scarcely two years old, travelling with a stranger, a man whom he has seen but for a day. Yet he left grandmother, and Kitty, and the old homestead, with only one little wail at parting, and now rides away munching his "fancy-cake" like a stoic. He plays, he chatters with his stranger friend, he lies down on the seat and sleeps, and when there is a stir among his colors and his friend says, "Waking up, Freddy?" Freddy pipes out his little "ish" cheerily, and rubs his little fist in his black eyes, and stares about content. I do not know, Freddy. Such equanimity is suspicious. Is it suppression or destitution of feeling? Is it your good training or your defective organization? Cry a little, Freddy, shy a little, Freddy, for very shame. I am afraid there is a cold little heart under your scarlet frock, and that by and by the cold little heart will grow and grow, — out of the memory of the scarlet frock, out of the sight of bright black eyes; and somewhere there will be a bad, hard man to wife and child. But let us not take time by the forelock.

And here, in a dingy little village, in the cold, clouded early morning, comes a Western woman, driving a two-horse wagon up to the dingy little station, with a baby in her arms, and another at her side. She sits in the wagon holding the horses, while her mother, an old, gray-headed woman, climbs out over the high wheel alone. She has come in that wagon, she tells us, more than seven miles before eight o'clock, through this comfortless morning, on her weary way, a hundred miles, to visit a sick daughter; and the other daughter, whose husband is also ill, must drive home alone with her babies. They are energetic women, and I praise their energy; but I do not praise that state of things which writes its story in deep lines of toil and anxiety on brow, and cheek, and lip. Until it can be helped we must bear it, but we have not learned our best life so long as we have weather-beaten faces of women.

And now we thunder over the vast plain nearing the great city of the West. The blue lake, lord at once and vassal, lies tranquil and splendid at her feet. The sun comes out to do her honor, and give us a triumphant entrance. Roof and spire and dome are gilded with his shining, and she sits proudly in a state befitting her royal name. It is the city of the future, holding out welcoming hands to the wanderers of the past. It is Peace and Plenty and Prosperity, crowned on their happy shore, inviting all comers to such princely cheer as changes want into wealth, and for the silence of stagnation gives songs of a thousand-stringed lyre.

But when you get into it! Lyre indeed! The word has an ominous echo. O my Queen, the diadem shines glorious on your brow, but woe is me for your draggled petticoats! Through slimy street after slimy street the sluggish train creeps on. The track is wellnigh buried in liquid mud. The unhappy houses are set down all straggling in a huge mud-puddle. The back yards are mire, and mire oozes up to the front door. Cholera! one might pray for its advent as an angel of mercy.

Through the Slough of Despond, the train trails reluctantly into a barn, as I judge in the dull twilight of noonday. There is no discoverable waiting-room, and we cross the city at once to the Milwaukee Station, and spend the laggard hours in a state of desperate homesickness, in a desolate, comfortless, cold room. A forbidding, leaden sky, cold, fierce winds, streets heavy with mud, cars, carriages, carts, steamer and sail-craft crammed together under the station windows, all struggling and all muddy; and when the struggle becomes too severe, the very bridges begin to writhe, and the whole earth seems a-squirm. And this is Chicago, and, alas! I know a girl who, besides being just married, must go to Chicago, and live all the days of her life! The longer we stay in this cheerless room, the more and more gloomy seems Chicago, and it spreads and spreads, and enshrouds the whole West. But here are the human beings that bring their own story with them. There is a pretty young Irish girl, with her tall, awkward, blushing bridegroom, not any more at ease for his unwonted black broadcloth and his high, stiff hat. They are both perfectly fresh, and life is full of new sensations. There is a family, — the father red-faced, sandy-haired, very ugly, deformed in one arm, defaced in one eye, and shabbily dressed, — the mother plain, and dressed with a sort of easy decency, as if she might have had finer clothes if she had chosen, but her clothes are good enough, — one bright little girl, and one baby. They have managed somehow to get at the heart of things. They are full of content. The husband and wife are absorbed in each other and in the children, without any silly or selfish demonstration of affection. The woman's position is exactly what it ought to be. She is the centre of interest, the motive power, the final cause. She constitutes the home. He is the strong wall round about, sheltering and fending. She is the fire on the hearth, warming and lighting. He takes care of the children with that wisdom that bespeaks habit and tact. He fondles the little one till it crows with delight. She looks on smiling, calm, and restful, and pleasant. He too is restful. He is at peace. They came together, not at first from any overpowering attachment, but both felt an inward yearning for home and care and love. Both had felt the world's rough side. Both were outwardly unattractive, and each was a little grateful as well as glad for the other's attention. They had the sense to discern each other's good qualities, and to appreciate the happiness of companionship and confidence. They learned to value each other, — yes, and to love each other, and are a thousand times happier than many who marry for love, but have not wisdom to see what love needs to keep its fires burning.

This is all theory, to be sure, but it is more true than many facts, and you might spend your time to worse account in a dismal railroad station.

There is another family group whom I fancy to be typical Western people, — father, mother, daughter, and granddaughter. They are comfortably and plainly, but not shabbily nor fashionably dressed. They are of country stock. They are not awkward, nor self-conscious, nor forward. They simply mind their own business and do not stare. (Neither do I! I am absorbed in lambs' tongues.) They are intelligent; they know what is going on in the world. They have a keen relish for and perception of humor, and a big tin luncheon-pail with a light cover, holding "goodies" enough to last a week, — chicken, and white bread, and pies. The grandmother is an invalid. Her pale, wasted face tells of suffering, but it is sweet, and motherly too, and it has by no means lost its shrewdness and its fun. The wife, her daughter, is tired and worn, but the fun is in her black eyes too. The father is pale and bent, but cheerful. They have had a hard life, but it has not been an unhappy one on the whole. Affection has warmed it, and a sense of the ludicrous has lighted and relieved it.

There is another old woman, with a prominent Roman nose, sharp chin, and eager, anxious eyes. The difference between the two old ladies is really striking. They are both in the same position in life; but one has character, the other has none. One is refined, the other unrefined, but nothing more, — not positively coarse, but without enough cohesion to take a polish. One would be at home and respected anywhere, the other nowhere. The latter is so full of anxiety that one pities her, and would gladly give her aid, but no aid avails. It is impossible to relieve her. Her restlessness is beyond reason. She attaches herself to every one that comes in. She has, as we say in the country, a finger in every pie. I saw her at first in company with the pleasant family, and supposed she belonged to them. The granddaughter came in bearing the invalid's pillow. "Here, set that down here," said the anxious old woman, with an air of being one of the family. When they lunched she drew up and lunched with them, but from her own bag. Of all that came in she asked the same question, in a harsh, dull, monotonous voice,—"You going to Milwaukee?" Generally she queried further, if they knew what cars they were going to take, and how they were going to know. She is in a fever lest the train should go without her, though assured that it is still two hours before the time of starting, and that we are all going in the same train. If a person on the other side of the room looks at his watch, she calls out to know what time it is, and if it is not most time to go. The young girl leaves the room, and she bids her be back soon, as it is most time to go. She thinks the husband is gone a long time, and tells the wife she is afraid she wont find her father! "O yes!" says the wife, with a smothered twinkle in her black eyes, "I think I shall be able to find *my father!*" She informs the assembly generally, without addressing any one in particular, that she is on her way to visit her daughter; that she is not accustomed to travelling, and has already gone one day wrong; but she is right now. She has to go from Chicago to Milwaukee, from Milwaukee to Sheboygan, and from Sheboygan to Wisconsin.

"Where in Wisconsin do you go?" asks some one disposed to assist her.

"Go from Chicago to Milwaukee, from Milwaukee to Sheboygan, and from Sheboygan to Wisconsin."

"Yes, but Sheboygan is in Wisconsin. When you get to Sheboygan, where do you go next?"

"Yes, that 's where I am going, — from Chicago to Milwaukee, from Milwaukee to Sheboygan, and from Sheboygan to Wisconsin. Yes."

Who can give help to such a muddled brain?

In due time the train is pushed up, and the station empties itself into the cars. "I should like to sit with you," says the old woman to the wife; but the wife intimates that she is hoping to have a seat by herself, and get a little sleep.

"Well, I'll sit on this side then." (Assuringly,) "I'll keep close to you!"

Up we go swiftly into Wisconsin. It rains and rains and rains; what is the weather thinking about? But the rain is drenching and downright and wholesome, not sulky and noncommittal; and there are hills and deep woods, a gentle, smiling verdure, a fresh, clear, pleasant country, and we take courage again. Even through the rain Wisconsin looks homelike, as if one might bring hither heartsomely his household gods; and I marvel why, with so much land in the country, it should have been thought advisable to tuck in Indiana and Illinois. They seem but huge quagmires, stale, flat, and unprofitable, that one must traverse from solid ground to solid ground. They could so well be spared from the face of the earth, and would agreeably simplify the geography.

But our anxious friend, who subsided a little when she was fairly in the car, is again rapidly working herself up into a violent ferment. At every station she asks her neighbor in front if this is Milwaukee. "O no! we shall not get to Milwaukee this long while." Straightway she appeals to her neighbor behind, "This is n't Milwaukee, is it?" And hardly waiting for a reply, she trots to the other side of the car to inquire eagerly if this is Milwaukee. After being told, perhaps six times, that it is not Milwaukee, she begins to harbor a suspicion that it is not, and trots back to her seat and places herself on the edge of it, with her hand on the back of the one in front, ready to start in case the village should pop up at any time and declare itself Milwaukee. Her semi-quiescence continues till the conductor comes in. Him she plies with questions by the time he stops within four feet of her. She improves the time while he is examining her ticket. She twists around, and continues the consultation till he is hopelessly past her. Then she springs up, and follows him down the aisle, talking in the same monotone till the door closes behind him, when she comes back murmuring abstractedly, "Milwaukee to Sheboygan, Sheboygan to Wisconsin," — and everybody looks at each other with a great show of sobriety. Whenever a new passenger enters she impresses him into her service. He thinks she is a lonely, unprotected woman, and kindly and impressively tries to make the route clear to her, to the amusement of the other passengers ; but he presently discovers the impracticability of his attempt, and quietly falls into the ranks of the initiated. "I 'm alone and I ain't accustomed to travelling," she occasionally meditates aloud, in her deep, hard, uncadenced voice.

"Yes," says another, making one more attempt to soothe her, for her trepidation is so extreme as to be quite pitiful, although so ridiculous ; "but there are plenty of people who know all about travelling, and they have promised to see that you get out and get in at the right places, and — "

"But they did n't tell me how I should go from Milwaukee to Sheboygan, and She — "

"Because you ask so many questions so many times that you become confused, and do not know what is said to you. Now " (soothingly) "you will be quite tired out if you keep walking around, and worrying all the time."

"Yes," from the very bottom of her poor old heart.

"Well, then, be quiet and rest till we get to Milwaukee, and you shall certainly be put safely on your way to Sheboygan."

And by the time her friendly adviser is fairly seated, I turn my head to see the evil spirit of unrest entering into the woman, and driving her down the aisle, head forward, in her bootless quest for Milwaukee.

When the baggage-agent enters the car, some one requests him to take charge of the wanderer. He may be a kind-hearted man and glad to do it, but if he is hard-hearted and loath he cannot very well help himself. She tells her story with zest, and he promises to take care of her. At the station a lively little colloquy springs up. One says the boat does not go, and the wanderer must stay at a hotel; another says the boat does go, and at any rate it is lying at the wharf, and she can stay on board; another says she should not be in Milwaukee at all, — that she should have taken boat at Grand Haven and gone directly across to Sheboygan; and a fourth affirms that she was right to come around, as it would not have been safe to cross the lake in such a storm; — all of which is very quieting to the disturbed lady. It is decided at length that she shall go to the boat, and the baggage-agent brings a man to take her thither. But she believes in the baggage-agent, and does not believe in the boatman, and with woman's devotion she clings to her first love. The first love, as is usual in such cases, finds her clinging decidedly troublesome, and has almost to push her away. Finally, the boatman walks off indifferently in one direction, the baggage-man in another, and the unhappy woman writhes a moment, turning towards each in an agony of doubt, but at length follows the boatman. My last picture of her is a silhouette: a man with a lantern, walking off with easy strides through the rain and the darkness; a woman hurrying after him, with long, uneasy strides, in lank, dripping skirts, — hurrying madly from Milwaukee to Sheboygan, and from Sheboygan to Wisconsin.

Girls, this is every word true, or rather every incident true. Be careful, then, to exercise what little sense you have while you are young, lest when you become old you find suddenly that you have no sense to exercise.

CHAPTER II.

Darwinian Theory in Milwaukee. — Milwaukee itself. — Pottawatomies in Newhall House. — Wonderful Advance of Civilization in Milwaukee. — Remarkable Girl in Milwaukee. — Saint Paul considered in his Relations to Milwaukee. — Aged Party in Train. — Motherless Baby in Train. — Treatise on the Inalienability of motherless Babies. — A Woman bringing a Man to Time. — Coming to Time herself. — A disagreeable Damsel. — General Moral Reflections on Railroad Accommodations. — Special Immoralities in Railroad Lack of Accommodations. — Model Conductor. — Superhumanly Model Conductor. — Evolving a Conductor from our Moral Consciousness. — Depicting a Conductor from Observation. — Laying down the (Higher) Law. — Constant changing of the Isothermal Lines in Railway Trains. — Raid upon the Ventilators. — Pitched Battle in the Train. — Defeat of the heaviest Battalions with great Slaughter. — Millennium on a Railroad. — A Beetle bewitched. — A terrible Infant. — An accomplished Young Lady. — Rose-colored Nuns. — Happy Teutons. — Fine Writing on the Mississippi River.

IN Milwaukee we are forcibly impressed with the growth and grandeur of the West. So favorable are the climatic conditions of that garden of America, that the mice run rank into rats. This is not fascinating to the traveller, still it is better than Albany and Niagara. Rats if not winning are tangible. I should not go so far as to make pets of them, as they do at the Newhall House; but I mention the fact of their transmutation as an interesting item of natural history, and an additional confirmation of the Darwinian theory of development. Here we have what has long been desired, — an actual example of the transmutation of species.

Milwaukee is a fair city in a fair country. It rains here all the time, but the rain comes down with spirit on clean pavements, and is spiritedly spattered back. The whole city looks hard and sound. It is built of the soft cream-colored brick which its own brick-kilns furnish, and it seems solid, old, durable.

It surprises me, this Milwaukee. Why, am I then antiquity? But I remember when Wisconsin was a Territory, and a Territory seemed a wild savage *terra incognita*, ravaged by "*Wín*nebagoes, *Win*nebagoes, *Pót*tawatomies, *Pót*tawatomies, *Sí*-oose, *Sí*-oose," as we used to repeat in concert, with swaying, sonorous sing-song. Yet here is a change from an ancient to a modern world. For Pottawatomies and Winnebagoes, is a huge hotel, are velvet sofas and chairs and carpets; small, social round tables in the dining-room, each one adorned with flowers; printed bills of a fare as profuse and varied and *recherché* as any in old Eastern cities, and as well cooked as in most of them; purple and scarlet and fine-twined linen. It is so extravagantly rainy that we cannot go out, but the obliging landlord — he must have been the landlord, for he lacked that polished and elaborate urbanity which distinguishes the hotel clerk, — besides he laughed heartily upon occasion, which would be deleterious to clerical dignity — the obliging landlord does his best to make up for it by taking us over his house, from turret to foundation-stone. Four hundred rooms have the Pottawatomies in which to bestow themselves; four hundred rooms, furnished, some with luxury and even elegance, all with decency and comfort, heated by steam, and provided with hot and cold baths. It might be conjectured that the Pottawatomies would stand afar off and dance a war-dance of surprise and admiration around the marvellous house; but we are assured that only last week they rushed in and filled all these rooms to overflowing, and, for aught that appears to the contrary, handled their napkins and flower-vases and bell-ropes and bath-tubs as decorously as Eastern savages. From the top of the house we behold the glory of the city, the fair young city, dimpling softly to her valleys, rising gently to her hills,—glory of church-spire and school-house, and the softer glory of happy homes. I see them shining dimly through the rain, draped with vines and warm with a cheerful glow. Taste and comfort and content are surely there, for energy alone could never make this Wisconsin wilderness blossom in such roses. A single fact well shows how rapidly the course of empire has taken its westward way. Only in 1840 there was but a single school in Milwaukee, with twenty-five scholars; now, there are three hundred lager-beer shops!

And there is a girl in Milwaukee, I do not know her name, of whom her male friends, chatting in the hotel parlor, speak thus: "She is accomplished, lively, agreeable, admirable,—why is she not married?"

"I think," says another, smiling, yet earnest, "it is because she is so intensely in love with her mother. You have only to start a conversation with either of them on the subject of the other, and they are eloquent."

This is high art and high nature in civilization,—an affection between parent and child so strong as to be absorbing and exclusive. For it will absorb nothing bad, will exclude nothing good. A heart so fixed will not be likely ever to loose its hold. Occupied already with a strong, pure love, it is in little danger of being dispossessed by a weak or worthless one. Nothing but integrity and courage and capacity, one would say, can enter there. Happy mother and happy daughter! Happy man, too, who shall one day come and see and conquer!

Away from Milwaukee, straight in among Sioux and Winnebagoes and Pottawatomies. Without, all is rain and darkness, tomahawks and scalping-knives and the smoky glare of pitch-pine torches; within, the mild glow of lamps, the satin-wood and velvet of civilization. Rushing through the night, to my eyes, gazing steadfastly forward seeing nothing, comes suddenly a quiver and fire in the curved letters above the car-door,—

Milwaukee and St. Paul.

Milwaukee and St. Paul. Late-born city of a

late-born continent, never dreamed of by Paul. A sleeping princess resting on the shores of her beautiful, broad lake, veiled in enchanted slumbers these eighteen hundred years, while Paul and his fifty generations have risen to the light and gone down to the darkness in an undisputed apostolic succession. Now she wakes from her lovely sleep, she fronts the ruddy dawn, and the sunlight of Paul's Holy Land touches her youthful brow with the splendor of the morning. What wizard hand has suddenly and silently bridged this gulf of time and space, and set the old name and the new side by side, in a union so harmonious and so obvious that the world sees, unastonished, and as though it had not seen?

Milwaukee and St. Paul. Does he know, I wonder, in his heavenly habitations, how green his memory lives in this new world? Does he see the strong city springing up in the wilderness, midway between two oceans, centre of a great and growing nation, centre of a far-stretching continent that rose from the undreamed solitude of the sea hundreds of years after his death, baptizing itself, in all its young vigor and its high hope, with the name of the martyr who died a death of violence and shame eighteen hundred years ago? And if he does know it, I wonder if he cares. Yes, as a martyr may, not as a Cæsar might.

Milwaukee and St. Paul. The very words are a lesson of honor and trust, of the futility of convention, of the immortality of principle. And sorely our young nation needs them in her headlong chase for good. Many men lived in Paul's day who wrought madly for earthly glory and honor and immortality, and history gives us not so much as the record of a name. Paul determined to know nothing among his generation save Jesus Christ and him crucified, and, throughout a world grown tenfold greater than Paul ever knew, his fame shines with a steady, serene, and ever-increasing brightness. Leaving house, and parents, and brother, and wife, and child, for the kingdom of God's sake, he has received manifold more in this present time, and in the world to come life everlasting.

There is an old couple in the car, husband and wife, well on towards seventy, another woman and a man, all strangers to each other, all grandfathers and grandmothers; nice, honest people, who never quarrelled with the existing order of things. They while away the time with a great deal of interesting, commonplace conversation, showing a remarkable unanimity of opinion. There is also a young man with an infant in his arms. He leaves the train at a way-station, and one of the company tells the other what he has gathered of the young man's story. His wife has died within a few weeks, and this baby is the youngest of four children. He has given it away to some one in this village where we are waiting. They all pity the poor child. One tender-hearted old woman has a great deal of feelin' for it. She knows how to sympathize. Her own daughter died, leaving a little child. They hope this child will be taken good care of. Probably it will, for it is going to live with a relative of its mother. It seems not to occur to any of them that there can be wrong in the father's giving away his child. I long to say to them: Good, kind people, fatherly men, motherly women, unseared consciences, what right has this man to give away this child? Whose child is it? His own. Held by no other title than that which makes his horse or house his? Will God receive from him a quitclaim deed as valid evidence of transfer? When God asks him at his judgment-day, "Where is the child I gave into thy hands?" will it be enough to answer, "I gave it away to my wife's cousin"? Can a man wash his hands of his child's blood so easily?

I know what they would say: "Why, the child will be a great deal better off than if he had kept it himself." So the child would be a great deal better off in heaven than on earth, but that would not justify him in drowning it. He has just as good a right to give it to the angels as he has to give it to men and women. The child is his, and is "not transferable." He ought to retain his power over it, and his love and care for it. That its mother is dead is the worst possible reason why it should lose its father too. When a man is deprived of his right arm, does he cut off his left? When the mother dies, the father's duty is, as far as possible, to be both father and mother to the children. If he fails then, he fails honorably, but he need not fail. Men have tried it and have succeeded. To fail without trying is shameful. A man can no more rightfully give away his child than he can give away his own soul. Recklessly we assume and recklessly relinquish the most solemn trusts, but God maketh inquisition. Poverty or disease may force the child from its father's arms, but this young man bore no marks of either. He was well-dressed and well-looking, and, as far as appearances go, perfectly able to take care of all four of his children if he had been willing to devote himself to them. Good people, you have so much pity for the young man! I have very little. I am a hard-hearted, evil-minded traveller, and it looks to me full as likely as anything else that he is merely clearing the decks for another engagement!

I think my old friends have reached the same conclusion, though probably by a different route; for when my ears are open again, the man is telling an up-country story to his sympathizing fellow-travellers. "There 's a man up in our town been courtin' a woman some time. She 's a school-teacher and smart. She was a widow and had two children. He 's got two children, too. Boys. One on 'em drives an omnibus, t' other sells papers and sich. Well, they take care o' themselves. When the thing had been goin' on perhaps a year, an' he thought he 'd got her pretty well hitched on, he kind o' talked round about the children, — asked her if she could n't put 'em out somewher. Well, the amount of it was he wanted her, but he did n't want the children. Well, I tell ye, she rared right up, and told him he might go to the devil! She wa'n't goin' to sacrifice her children for him nor no other man! Bet ye, he come to time quick!"

A good story if he had only stopped there, but he did not. He rubbed his hands and laughed, and shuffled his feet, and then added in an indifferent tone, as if it were of no especial moment, only a thing to be expected, — "*And they 're married now!*"

At midnight we leave the land and trust ourselves to the Great River. The steamer Damsel is our doom, and a very slatternly and unmannerly damsel she turns out to be. In the first place, the boat is crowded and we can get no state-rooms, not, however, because of the crowd, but of our blind confidence in a mendacious officer. In the next place, the fire in the stove is low, and the big, swaggering boy rekindles it with kerosene. The passengers shivering around the stove remonstrate, (not I, — I would rather run the risk of being blown up,) but he laughs, and says it is nothing but a little water, and gives another flirt to his can. Half a dozen times, at least, the kerosene can is brought forward, and the oil, not poured, but flung upon the fire. The flames flare out of the door and leap half-way up to the ceiling. A man appeals to one of the officers, who says there is no danger. All the talk about kerosene exploding is nothing. It is harmless as water. They have always used it, and never had any trouble. In spite of oil and wood, we are wretchedly uncomfortable. There are draughts everywhere, and we take violent colds. The way they open state-rooms on board the Damsel is to boost a boy to the top of the door, then make him wriggle through the ventilator, a somewhat prolonged process, and loose the fastenings from the inside. At least, that is the way I saw it done, and an edifying spectacle it is. The table is set with a warm, greasy abundance. There is an indefinable sham splendor all around, half disgusting and wholly comical. The paint and gilding, the velvet and Brussels, the plate, and the attendants show bravely by lamp-light, but the honest indignant sun puts all the dirty magnificence to shame. The crew are negroes, ragged, filthy, roistering, insubordinate, inefficient, and profane to the last degree. The orders are noisy, wordy, and undignified, given as a rollicking boy might order his comrades over whom he had no command, rather than as an officer to his men. The negroes re-issue them one to another with comments, questions, and expletives, and obey them in their own time and way. Wrestling, fighting, and swearing are their business; running the boat their interruption. The luggage and freight are their playthings, which they pull and kick about with a more hearty good-will than they take to anything else. Five men make the noise of a hundred, and possibly do the work of one. Repeatedly we get aground, and are pushed off with poles. The only wonder is that we get on at all with such utter recklessness and mismanagement. All the while our Floating Palace is unspeakably dirty, and we assimilate to it more and more. These evils are entirely unnecessary, or I should not speak of them. The inconveniences of real frontier life may make a part of its attractiveness; but here is no frontier life; here are simply three days of vile discomfort that might just as well be delight, were it not for gross and wanton negligence or cupidity, or both. When we came back down the river we came in the steamer Chippewa (I think was the name), run, I believe, in opposition to the regular railroad line. It made the distance in less than half the time. The fare was three dollars less than that of the Damsel. The boat was clean, the crew so quiet that there hardly seemed to be any crew, and the voyage an unalloyed pleasure. It was simply that, in the one, all things were done decently and in order; in the other, all things were done indecently and in disorder. In the one case a little attention was shown to the comfort and safety of the passengers; in the other, both seemed to be left quite out of the account.

I suppose that the present style of railway management is just as good for the healthy development of a country as any other, or wise and energetic men who desire the development of a country would change it. People, it is found, will travel, whether they travel comfortably or uncomfortably. If a man desires to go West to make his fortune, he will go, whether he is treated with civility or incivility on the road, whether his carriage be warm or cold, and his surroundings clean or unclean. And as it is, perhaps, cheaper on the whole for a corporation to disregard these small matters than it is to regard them, probably there is no use in saying anything about them. But though in the struggle for life one cannot stand upon trifles, it is very certain that in travelling for pleasure one's opinion of a country is largely influenced by just these trifles. And very justly too, for it is in little things that civilization shows itself. It is the finger-nails rather than the fineness of the broadcloath by which you judge the man. Barbaric splendor may consort with barbaric rudeness. A journey from the sea-coast to the interior shows plainly enough whence come those unpleasant books which British tourists have from time to time written about America. To a foreigner, the temptation to ridicule and vilify a country which lays itself so fearfully open to ridicule and vilification must be wellnigh irresistible. He may feel that it is no more than strict poetic justice for him to take out in fun what has been taken out of him in fare. Moreover, the disagreeable traits are thrust directly and continually upon his notice, are perpetually interfering with his personal comfort, while the excellences are more remote and abstract, and as most travellers are superficial and selfish, like the rest of us, we get irritable and irritating books, and much bad blood. But to a countryman it is too serious a matter to be made a jest of. It involves personal shame and blame. I do not know how our own compares with other countries; we may be on a higher plane than any in the Old World, but for all that our plane is low. The foulness of some — of many — of the steam-cars was such as one shudders to remember. Many of the slips it was impossible to enter, so filthy had the floor been made by their previous occupants. Even when you were able to secure a decent one, it would often happen that the nasty habits of the men around would render your position absolutely sickening. Railroad companies have instituted the smoking-car and the ladies' car, — very good as far as it goes. But the ladies' car is not reserved for women. Men are allowed to enter it if they accompany women. I suppose it was assumed that a woman would be the man's guaranty for good behavior. Pity it is not so; but, spite of wife or child, men bring with them their unclean lips and defile a whole car, while a man of perfect purity, if he happen to be alone, must be shut out into what horror of great darkness the imagination fails to portray. If, instead of a ladies' car, we could have a clean car, the arrangement would be far more agreeable.

Nor should I say that the railroads of the West are characterized by the civility of their servants. I should say quite the contrary, were it not that generalization on data so imperfect as mine is worthless, even if its statements happen to be true. Moreover, civility is perhaps not altogether a matter of latitude and longitude, but of individuals and even of moods as well. Perhaps a Western man travelling in the East might make the same remark concerning Eastern railroads that I should be inclined to make concerning his. The fault is not so much an aggressive incivility as a lack of civility, — an indifference to the common courtesies which distinguish savage from civilized life. No reasonable person would demand so much attention as some conductors give. I remember one, on the road between Cleveland and Toledo, who looked after his passengers as if they had been his family, taking us from a cold to a warm car, seeing that wet shawls and wraps were thoroughly dried, bringing in his books to study out the most desirable routes, and finally burdening himself with all the feminine hand-baggage he could carry, in aiding our passage from his own to another train. There was another conductor on the train from Chicago to Indianapolis, — a man whose good-nature was something noteworthy in life, not to say a steam-car. His patience and benevolence were inexhaustible. It was a regularly recurring pleasure to see his beautiful face come shining through the car. He rendered no especial, tangible service, but he was interested and friendly. When he took your tickets it was as if he had given you the right hand of fellowship, and sworn to stand by you through thick and thin. I saw him afterwards when off duty. He came into the train and met his family, — a pretty, lively, loving little woman, two little girls, and a baby, — and he held the baby all the way, and played with it, and chatted with his wife, and looked as happy as he deserved to be, — and she looked as happy as the wife of such a man should look. And I sat behind them, and thought, if I were the Pope, I would sprinkle holy water over them, and lay my hand on their heads and pronounce a benediction!

But such conductors are a gift of the gods. We may welcome them when they come, but not clamor for them when they are withheld. Yet surely it is not unreasonable to ask that conductors shall be able and willing to give information as to times and ways of travel on their own roads. There are often points concerning the arrival and departure of trains, which materially affect a person's plans, and which a conductor might settle in two minutes, — in ten seconds. Yet, not unfrequently, questions are so imperfectly and unsatisfactorily answered, that they might as well not be answered at all. For instance, we are discussing whether we shall stop in Chicago for the night, or go through to

Milwaukee. We appeal to the conductor to know if we change cars in Chicago. "We do," is the hurried reply, with such a *noli me tangere* air, that no ordinary valor can brave another question. After settling down for a night's ride, we learn by chance that not only do we change cars at Chicago, but stations also, and moreover the train arriving at ten in the evening does not leave till six in the morning; so that we can get neither a night's sleep nor a night's travel, and are obliged as the next best resort to be set down in Mudhole. It never was my way to suffer in silence, and it is a satisfaction to know that one conductor has been enlightened as to his duty in such cases; but if one tenth part of the time which he spent afterwards in explaining why he had not answered the question properly had been spent in answering it at the time of it, there would have been a good deal of trouble saved on both sides. As I said, this seems not to proceed from any premeditated incivility, but from mere inattention to or unconsciousness of the proprieties of the situation. Doubtless, a conductor, from New Year's to Christmas, is asked many unnecessary and silly questions. Doubtless, also, many questions which seem to him unnecessary and silly are not so to the questioner. But no matter if they are. We are told by high authority that the fools are three out of four in every person's acquaintance, so that a large majority of the travelling public are foolish, and as railroads are theoretically, at least, for the convenience of the public, and not for the emolument of the stockholders, provision should be made for any questions which travellers ask in good faith, as necessary to the successful prosecution of their journey. To a person who goes into Chicago every day, it may be impossible to conceive a fatuity so great as not to know that Chicago is a point of departure, and not a mere place of transit; yet such fatuity does exist, and should be taken into account. This one thing, it seems to me, is very apt to fall out of sight not in the West alone, that railroads are created for people, and not people for railroads; and that the officers of a railroad are public servants and not irresponsible monarchs.

In nearly all the cars in which we travelled, there was a stove and a fire, indicating an original benevolent intention; but the fire was constantly going out, — three times for example in one trip from one to twelve in the evening. The agreeable and healthful consequence was a temperature ranging from the red-hot shimmer of an air-tight to the shivering zero of no fire at all, — a change not beneficial to the strong, but absolutely dangerous to the weak. There are usually arrangements for a degree of ventilation, but it seems to be nobody's business to see that these arrangements are carried into effect. We entered a car one morning from the fresh stinging air. We found a hot fire, a full carriage, every ventilator shut, and, of course, a horrible condition of things; but nobody seemed to mind it. It was suggested to the conductor that the ventilators might be opened, "Why, yes, certainly, he should think so," and he sprang at them briskly with great good-nature. But they resisted his efforts with a stubbornness that indicated long disuse. He called in the brakeman; one or two passengers volunteered their services; and, arming themselves with poker, and shovel, and billets of wood, they made such a vigorous onset that the ventilators soon gave way, and we had a fine current of sweet air rushing through the car, and driving out the sluggish death that had been slowly settling down upon us.

As we were approaching Chicago, one of those omnibus men who go through a train seeking whom they may devour scattered some of his tickets to our party. When he had gathered them up again, he coolly remarked that he would take the other ticket. There was no other ticket forthcoming. He insisted that one had been retained. He was assured to the contrary, but he "believed what he saw with his own eyes." What he saw with his own eyes was an Eastern horse-car ticket, of the same color as his own, in my half-open purse. Willing to satisfy him, I showed it to him; and invited him to examine the purse for himself. I think he saw that he was wrong, yet had not the manliness to apologize, and refused also to look into the purse, but muttered his belief again. Now I suppose one might survive a suspicion of theft. Every man has his price, but no one likes to be rated cheaply. Had it been a ticket to a coach and eight cream-colors, with footman and outriders, I might have been supposed actuated by laudable ambition, though pushed somewhat to extremes; but to be thought capable of stealing a ride in a cold, rickety, jolting omnibus, with a snarl of straw on the floor, was not to be tolerated. People speak about losing temper, as if all you can do with your temper is to lose it. But if, instead of losing temper you use it, — bring it up in full force, hold it well in hand, and hurl it straight and steady at your foe, it becomes a very effective weapon. I know that it made of my ticket-man a ticket-of-leave man in an incredibly short space of time. When the conductor came in he was regaled with the narrative. It was the same odd, droll, good-natured little man who led the charge on the ventilators. He seemed to think it a wondrous good joke, laughed an irresistible, deprecating, hearty little smothered laugh, and hoped we did not blame *him*. O no! but what was the man's name? Well, he was sure he did n't know. He came on the cars. Believed they called him Bob. That was all he knew about him. It was suggested to him whether his train would not make quite as good time without such bobs appended, — which seemed to amuse him mightily. But if nameless and irresponsible Bobs are to be allowed to infest trains and insult passengers at will, it is a question whether we shall not introduce the summary Southern style of procedure. A friend from South Carolina had the misfortune to lose his ticket. To our condolence, he replied quietly that he should not pay again.

"But what will you do?"

"Tell the conductor I have lost it."

"And suppose he does not believe you?"

"O, I shall knock him down."

Now we shall have railroads properly conducted. The safety and comfort of the passengers will no longer be left to the character or caprice of individuals, but the conduct of trains will be reduced to a system, of which civility will be a component part. Placidity of temper will be tested in competitive examinations. Due notice will be given before trains leave those edifying stations at which they are announced to stop from five to twenty minutes "for refreshments," and from which they are accustomed to slip away at their own sweet will, without so much as saying, "By your leave." Classification will be so strictly enforced, that even the engine will puff his smoke on the inoffensive side, and no hint of anything obnoxious shall come betwixt the wind and our nobility. So potent is the pen over the passions and the prejudices of corporations!

All this while we are sailing — when we are not aground — up through storm and night, the wild darkness and the gray morning twilight. We are a rough set on board this wretched Damsel. We have velvet chairs, but unwashen hands. We huddle around the stove, a dark, dingy cloud. The woman next me is a study, — short, sinewy, brown, with full, protruding mouth, prominent dark teeth, very conspicuous when she talks, and she talks much and confidentially to me. She wears a man's dark straw hat, with a red plaid ribbon tied around it in a home-made bow. She looks like a man herself, and acts not unlike a man, for she has been smoking her pipe vigorously on deck. She tells me she is going up into Minnesota somewhere, to visit her father and mother. He is over ninety years old. Her sister and daughter are also married, and living there, and want her to come; but her man wants her to go up and see how she likes it before he buys. Her father says he misses her. He ain't no company now to smoke with, and he misses Ann. When he lived with her they often used to get up in the night and have a smoke, and then go back to bed again. She has to smoke on account of her stomach. She talks about her boy, and is afraid he did n't get no sleep last night, and will be sick this morning. Her "boy" soon comes to view, a black-bearded lounging fellow, six feet high at least, and that little woman talks to him and of him as if he were only five years old. She is captain of her ship beyond question. She presently draws a small bottle from her pocket, takes a draught, and then, on hospitable thoughts intent, offers it to me. She says it is essence of peppermint, and she has wind in her stomach, and if she did not drink it she should faint. I am afraid I shall faint if I do. So I assure her I am perfectly well, and will not draw upon her small resources. She takes it in good part, and sticks to me through the journey with her pipe, and her plans, and her pa, and her exposed teeth. Altogether she impresses me as a good-natured fiend, — a little grinning, social imp, — as I tell her in mental apostrophes while listening to her confidences. A horrible woman. A woman? A beetle. A cockroach.

There is an unhappy child shrieking around the cabin. His straight yellow hair hangs over his forehead nearly to his eyes. He has a cold, cross, red face, raw nose, and his little bare legs above his low stockings are mottled and red. There is a possible heaven in his blue eyes, but he is going away from it every day under the guiding hand of his mother. I suppose the poor child is really wretched from cold; but he has a bad disposition besides, which manifests itself in incessant squalls, with or without provocation. I see him presently stray to the outside, and climb up the guards of the boat, and I rather hope he will tumble overboard. Certainly he might go farther and fare worse. There is a young Middle-State woman, tall, and slender, and shrewd, with a pleasant, liquid voice, an easy way of meeting everybody, and very indistinct notions of geography. She makes acquaintance right and left without leaving her arm-chair. She supposes the captain found travelling here very different during the war from what it is now. No, not materially, he says. But he must have had a good many shots from the guerillas! And she is not startled out of her easy self-satisfaction at being told that the guerillas never ventured up into the wilds of Wisconsin. We have a company of nuns on board, and they are by far the most intelligent and refined-looking people here. For one thing they are clean, and the eye dwells delighted and refreshed on their pure muslin and black and drab. Moreover they are quiet, and they are pretty; they ask no questions, they move about softly, their faces have repose. They are a little oasis in this desert. Sometimes a priest comes up, — there are three or four on board, — and they chat pleasantly and laugh heartily. There is a party of German girls going up to St. Paul, healthy, happy, homely, and no dirtier than the rest of us. They soon get on exceeding good terms with the servants, and I hear a couple just on the other side of the door arranging a correspondence. Flirt away, my hearties. Dan Cupid is no disdainer of humble folk, and disports himself as gayly among barnyard fowls as among birds of paradise.

But the twilight seems to be departing. There is a glimmer as of sunlight on the ceiling. We quickly take the hint, wrap ourselves warmly, and go on deck. Is it magic? Is it miracle? The dirty Damsel disappears, crew and cargo. At once and forever we know the Great River. Father of Waters, King of Waters, God's own hand has set the crown upon his forehead, and he reigns by right divine. So grand, so still, there is no speech nor language. Through night and storm we have sailed into another world. Here walk the Immortals, — nay, it is as if God himself — Jehovah of old — came down to tread these solitudes, and the hush of His awful presence lingers still.

God is here, but it is man's world. More sweet in its beauty, more solemn in its sublimity, more exultant in its splendor, than imagination ever conceived, — for us it is and was created. No puny meddlers we thrid this glorious wilderness, but heirs we enter upon our estate, all breathless with the first unfolding of its magnificence. Up the broad, cold, steel-blue river we wind steadily to its Northern home. No flutter of its orange groves, no fragrance of its Southern roses, no echo of its summer lands, can penetrate these distances. Only prophecies of the sturdy North are here, — the glitter of the Polar sea, the majesty of Arctic solitudes. The imagination is touched. The vision becomes continental. The eye looks out upon a hemisphere. Vast spaces, lost ages, the unsealed mysteries of cold and darkness and eternal silence sweep around the central thought, and people the wilderness with their solemn symbolism. Prettiness of gentle slope, wealth and splendor of hue, are not wanting, but they shine with veiled light. Mountains come down to meet the Great River. The mists of the night lift slowly away, and we are brought suddenly into the presence-chamber. One by one they stand out in all their rugged might, only softened here and there by fleecy clouds still clinging to their sides, and shining pink in the ruddy dawn. Bold bluffs that have come hundreds of miles from their inland home guard the river. They rise on both sides, fronting us bare and black, layer of solid rock piled on solid rock, defiant fortifications of some giant race, crowned here and there with frowning tower; here and there overborne and overgrown with wild-wood beauty, vine and moss and manifold leafage, gorgeous now with the glory of the vanishing summer. It is as if the everlasting hills had parted to give the Great River entrance to the hidden places of the world. And then the bold bluffs break into sharp cones, lonely mountains rising head and shoulders above their brethren, and keeping watch over the whole country; groups of mountains standing sentinel on the shores, almost leaning over the river, and hushing us to breathless silence as we sail through their awful shadow. And then the earth smiles again, the beetling cliffs recede into dim distances, and we glide through a pleasant valley. Green levels stretch away to the foot of the far cliffs, level with the river's blue, and as smooth, — sheltered and fertile, and fit for future homes. Nay, already the pioneer has found them, and many a hut and cottage and huddle of houses show whence art and science, and all the amenities of human life, shall one day radiate. And even as we greet them we have left them, and the heights clasp us again, the hills overshadow us, the solitude closes around us. All day long we pass through this enchanted wilderness. Frowning and smiling, advancing, receding, hill whispers to hill its secret over our heads; now across the valley-lands between it calls aloud, and now it lifts its forehead to the sky, rapt in its eternal thought. And the brilliance of clear mid-day, the golden haze of the afternoon, the lingering softness of twilight, and the moon's unclouded brightness woo out every form and shade of beauty, reveal every line of grandeur, deepen all the glooms and heighten all the lustres, till the soul is bewildered and wellnigh overpowered. Then welcome, brooding shelter of the night, kindly darkness that soon shall shape and shadow overflow! Welcome, sweet familiar twinkle of the old stars, beckoning us back to the world we knew before,—more home-like and more near than the home-lights gleaming on these strange shores!

CHAPTER III.

Parting Blessing. — On the Prairie. — Sublimity of a Minnesota Farm — A Violent Supposition. — The Bearing ot the Earth's Rotundity on Minnesota Farmers. — Flemish Painting of our House. — Elegant Extracts from Antique Rhymes. — Bill of Fare. — Bill of Costs. — Self-Help. — Second Self-Help. — Outdoors. — Farm Buildings. — Hard Work, and a good Deal of it. — Mitigating the Curse by Machinery. — Praiseworthy attempts at Description. — Sentiment hovering over a Threshing-Machine. — A Fling at the "lower States" in the Interest of Minnesota. — Many Things. — Computing the Gains. — Counting the Cost.

MINNESOTA. We have persevered, following the Great River through all its winding way. We have hugged now this shore and now that, seeking the tortuous channel. We have circled our last island, swept around our last curve, and now the prow points to land. There are no wharves. The bank glides gently down to take us, the Damsel thrusts her uncanny nose gently into the gravel, and we step ashore. Good by, Damsel.

May you sink a thousand fathoms deep or ever I set foot on your horrid deck again! May forty snags crash your timbers and drag you down into the turbid depths! May you blow up with kerosene when no passengers are on board! — as to officers and crew I make no stipulations. May you run aground and stick fast, and snap every pole that you try to push off with! May you be overthrown by wild winds on the eastern shore of Lake Pepin, and never heard of more! May every raft butt you, and every big steamer run you down, and every little steamer outstrip you! May water drown you, and fire burn you, and your sky rain thick disasters, till you cease to be a pestilent speck on the bosom of the River of Greatness!

River of Greatness! Country of Greatness! The thirty-one-hundred-mile-stretching stream kindles the land to emulation, and everything in Minnesota is on the magnificent scale. Standing at a cottage door the country reaches away like the sea. The horizon is regular and far. Broad sweep of field rises to meet broad sweep of sky. The earth rounds up under the heavens palpably, and as you drive across the broken prairies it is like driving across a brown, billowy ocean, rolling as far as the eye can see. A snarl of roads intersects the prairie, every man making a highway whithersoever he will. To the stranger eye it is a labyrinth in which one might be ensnared forever. But a certain instinct seems to guide the natives, and we constantly meet them driving along as quietly as if a stone wall on each side, after the New England fashion, kept them where they belong. Yet it hardly seems possible that they can know where they are going. Where we are going is to a Minnesota farm, — a Minnesota farm, where tradition says they look askance at bread and milk, counting nothing less than bread and cream a dish to set before the king. Now, Minnesota farming, I have discovered, is something altogether different from Massachusetts farming, — as much as the Mississippi is a different thing from the Merrimack. It is large, it is comprehensive, it is — well, it is rather sublime! It hardly comes within the scope of possibility that a man who had broadened to the wastes of Minnesota could ever come back and be content with the little pocket farms of New England. There are also, I judge, more of what are called "book-farmers." They do not go on there in the old ways in which their fathers trod, for the very good reason that they had neither ways nor fathers. They have broken ground for themselves, and they strike out independently. They make experiments, for they must make them. Indeed, their farming is itself an experiment. Their broad lands necessitate broad vision. They farm with their brains as well as with their hands. Rather, they bring their brains to bear on their hands, and piece them out with iron and steel to clasp their widening farms. If I might appropriate and alter a rustic phrase, I should say they substitute wheel-grease for elbow-grease. Instead of taking his hoe and going to work, the Minnesota farmer harnesses his horse and takes a drive; but his drive does a great deal more hoeing than the Massachusetts man's hoe.

Let us make believe now that we are so delighted with Minnesota, that we are going there to live, — and to get a living. We are young and strong, with muscles in our bodies, and skill in our fingers, and brains in our skulls, — and, let us say, with money in our pockets. For without money of what use is it to go anywhere? And yet every one says, — and it seems to be proved by observation and experience, — that the West is pre-eminently the place for poor men. There is plenty of land at government price, which is almost nominal, and there is also plenty of time to pay it in. Many who came with money are now poorer than those who had nothing when they arrived. We will therefore give away our money, that we may have no drawbacks to our prosperity, and buy a farm.

Minnesota, fortunately for us, is made on purpose for farms. It is cut up into sections, each containing a square mile; only, as the earth is round and grows smaller of girth from the equator to the poles, and as all measurements must mind the meridians whatever becomes of farmers, every now and then must be a man who loses a foot or two from his acres; but he has so much left that he does not mind it. Every sixteenth of these sections is appropriated — God bless our native land! — to the school-fund. By looking into Greenleaf's Arithmetic you will find that a square mile contains six hundred and forty acres, — a very pretty plat to be master of. Let us therefore imagine ourselves masters of it. Many farmers in Minnesota devote themselves to the raising of a single crop, — principally wheat. Others think this not the best way. One crop will run farms out, they say. They believe all land is improved by a rotation of crops, and they approve of raising a little corn, a little hay, a few hogs, a few sheep, a few apples. We believe also in a rotation of crops, especially sheep. We will select a farm well adapted to sheep-grazing. It has fine low level lands, and gentle hills, and a stream of clear, cold water running through it. On the southern slope our house shall be set square to the sun. It is for comfort, for present use, not for show; but it is a mistake to suppose that one can be comfortable without the decencies of life. Civilization is not so deeply rooted in any of us, that we can afford to dispense with outside helps. And because we are going out upon the prairies, we need not live in a shanty or between bare walls. Moreover, it is cheaper in the long run to cultivate ourselves as well as our farms, and not very much costlier in the short run. Besides, our benevolent predecessor has left us a house ready to hand. It has four rooms on the lower floor, a sitting-room, perhaps fourteen feet by fourteen, facing the south; on the other side of the front door a bedroom, behind these two front rooms, another bedroom, and a kitchen. Every room has at least two windows on two sides, for sunshine is an eminent adornment. Our sitting-room has light, cheerful paper, hung by its owners, and a stout, woollen carpet which their own hands made and nailed down. A few engravings give outlooks through the walls. A bracket in the corner holds a vase, and the vase holds an abundance of wild flowers and grasses. There is a writing-desk, book-shelf, or what-not by the window, and you shall find in a Minnesota book-case on the prairie such books as Household Friends, Imitation of Christ, Memoir of Margaret Fuller, Somerville's Physical Geography, Parker's Philosophy, Swedenborg's Christian Religion, Snow-Bound, Longfellow's Poems, Our Old Home, Christina Rosetti, and so on, — good company on prairie or in city. The bedrooms are large and airy. The kitchen has a pump in the sink. Opening from the sitting-room, and close to the kitchen, is a pantry, or store-room. It contains a dish cupboard, a crockery cupboard, one also for glass and silver, a shelf for the box of knives and forks, shelves for all sorts of cooking utensils, compartments with tight covers for rye-meal, wheat-flour, corn-meal, Graham meal, and bran, a closet for cold meats, milk shelves, a shelf for the water-pail, one also for dish-washing, and a hanging shelf before the window. So, dear Lady Una, you can stand in this store-room and prepare your meats, bread, pies, and other edibles for cooking, without leaving your place. You have only to turn around and you can lay your hand upon everything you want. Moreover, as your sitting-room is warmed by an air-tight, with an oven and a teakettle aperture, in the winter you can do nearly all your daily cooking here, and live as our homely dear old grandmothers used to say, —

> "As snug
> As a bug
> In a rug."

When our dinner is cooked it is of the nicest. Bread light and white, made of flour ground from wheat, which our own soil fattened; chicken-pie made of a prairie chicken, that came swooping down from the sky into our own yard; custards milked from our own cows and laid by our own hens,—at one or two removes; jellies that hung quivering on our own wild plum-trees;—everything cooked delicately. The table is set with fine white linen, with napkins and silver forks and spoons, and pretty, plain ware; really one might do worse than dine at a prairie farm-house. A building like this, erected when lumber was nine or ten dollars a thousand, say three years ago, cost not quite two hundred and fifty dollars. But then a great deal of ingenuity was built into it. For blinds, the owner obtains a model, and then makes them and paints them himself. He also washes or stains the outside of the house to some harmonious tint. He papers the rooms. He stains all the interior wood-work with a home-made preparation. Many of the doors and some of the window-frames are the work of his own hands. He lays the floor, and lathes the walls. He makes the little porch over the front door. All the cunning workmanship of the store-room is his. The dining-table, and the brackets, and scores of little contrivances, and even elegances, are the product of his mind, and hand, — aided by another mind as fertile, and other hands only less strong, not less skilful. From these other hands come the rustic frames for the engravings, the warm-looking curtains, and many a nameless but useful and pretty device. From both pair of hands come the large and comfortable lounge, with its piled-up cushions; it is not the work of a day or of a week, but of many winter evenings and many rainy mornings, — the gathered fragments of odd hours; and so first and best we have a home in the wilderness, and a home that will be constantly growing more home-like.

For our door-yard we have thousands of acres. A few trees are growing on the sheltered slope in front, and the sheltered slope behind is our garden. Here are our tomatoes, our sweet-corn, our beans and peas, our pie-plant, which remains fresh and tender and fit for cooking all summer long, our trellis-work for vines, our lilacs, and whatever we can coax to take root. And on fine summer days we throw wide open the front door and the back door, and the door between living-room and kitchen, the three doors being in one line, and prairie and garden catch pleasant looks at each other, and fling many a fragrant whisper through the house. But the garden is an aftergrowth. There are other things to be looked to. Especially is it a first requisite to get the farm well fenced in. A barn does not seem to be so indispensable to a farm as we have been accustomed to consider it. Few good barns are to be seen, though they are now coming more into use, as farmers have money and time to build them. The stable must come first. A very rude and primitive one gives shelter to the horses, who are nearly as important to the farm as the farmer himself. Crotched posts are set in the ground, the sides boarded, poles and rails laid across the top, the threshing-machine driven up alongside, and the straw-carrier heaps up the straw on them to form the roof. Sheds are made for the sheep in a similar manner, and are about four feet high. They open on the south. On the north side stacks of straw and hay are ranged so as to shelter the yard, and they give a very cosey look to the out-door establishment. As we have time, we join house and barn with a shed for the farm-wagons and machines, a wood-house, and a carpenter's shop. Then we are well protected against the north winds, and well open on the sunny southern side.

For our farming work: we begin by break ing ground in the spring, just as the green grass starts. The ploughing will be easier if we first burn off the dead grass. We can begin by the middle of May, and keep at it till the last of July. Then the field lies till the next spring. The native sod is so tough that we cannot do much with it the first year. The next spring having come, as soon as the frost gets out enough to let us cover the grain well, we sow it. The earlier the better. The crop is surer, and the grain of a better quality. If frost comes afterwards, or even snow, there is no harm done. The hardy little kernels have the inside track, and laugh at the feeble efforts of an effete winter. We do not sow by hand, as they do in picture-books, but with a broadcast sower. With two horses we go over from ten to fifteen acres a day. An ingenious little arrangement tells how much grain we put into the acre, and how many acres we go over, with as much accuracy as a time-clock tells the hours and minutes. If we find we are putting in too much or too little, we can adjust the machine to a different quantity, as readily as a clock is regulated. Three bushels of oats or one bushel and a half of wheat is the ordinary allowance to an acre. The machine sows and partially covers the grain. When it is new ground, we go over it two or three times with a harrow, and then we give it in charge to sunshine and rain and dew and air till the harvest-time.

We have also what we call sod corn and sod potatoes. We simply thrust an axe and a spade in between the sods, drop the corn, and cover it with the heel; but it does not yield the best crop. For sod potatoes we plough one furrow, and plant the potatoes in it about eighteen inches apart, and close to the land side, then plough another furrow which covers them. The potatoes come up between the sods. Then we plough three furrows and drop another row of potatoes. In this manner we get our best crop of potatoes. They need no hoeing. The land is necessarily free from weeds, for there are no seeds for the weeds to spring from. In breaking this ground, the shallower we plough the better. We want our furrow only two and a half or three inches deep. In harvest-time we plough as at planting. That turns the sod over and throws up the potatoes. We have three or four men or boys to follow and gather the potatoes which we have unearthed. We have now not only an excellent crop of potatoes, but we have the land in a better condition for next year's wheat crop than if we had not planted the potatoes. Now then, my statistician, what is the net gain on our potatoes?

But while we have been talking about the potatoes, May and June and July have been busy in our fields, and the wheat has ripened. We know neither sickle nor cradle here, but we bring up the horses and the header. The header aims straight at the heads of the wheat, designing to get only as much straw as is necessary in order to secure all the heads. It leaves the stubble from one and a half to two feet high. A man steers the machine with a rudder, as you steer a boat. The rudder is a castor wheel. The horses are harnessed in behind the header, and move it like a wheelbarrow, and cannot go wrong. They have simply to go wherever the header is steered. A header has four horses abreast, two on each side of the tongue. It often cuts twenty-two acres a day, sometimes thirty; the average is about eighteen. The slightest rain stops work. The machine clogs, and grain must not be stacked while damp. The header is accompanied by three racks, and each rack has two horses and a driver. The header-rack is a floor or platform on wheels, with sides of canvas, to catch the grain thrown from the header. We begin our harvesting in July. We first find the centre of our big lot, then steer our header straight for that centre, cutting a swath as we go ten feet wide. Our rack is on the left of the header, and when we first enter, of course we have to trample the grain sadly. But why, O extravagant Western Farmer, do you not send a man in beforehand to cut down a swath with his own right arm, and so save all the trampling? "Oh!" says my lord, "when we are working with fourteen men and ten horses, it won't do to bother about a handful of wheat." So they laugh to scorn our contracted New England ideas of economy. Having gained the centre, the header, and its devoted wife, the rack, go round in as small a circle as possible, say two or three rods in circumference, and then begin to stack. The grain when cut by the header is thrown by an endless apron, revolving like a belt, into the header rack on its left. This apron is about thirty feet long. It is made of stout canvas cloth, with strips of wood affixed crosswise to carry up the straw. The header rack must keep close up under the spout of the header. When one rack is full, it deposits its load in the centre of the field, while another rack drives up immediately and takes its place on the left of the header. One man stands on the rack to load, jumping from rack to rack as each fresh one comes up. There is one man to stack, and another to trim up the stacks. The stacks are made twenty-five or thirty feet long, and nine or ten feet wide, and symmetrically curved and shaped. They are generally arranged in groups of four, each group containing two or three hundred bushels of wheat. They are often made on a knoll or the poorest part of the field, and the straw lies there till it rots or is burnt, and so enriches the soil.

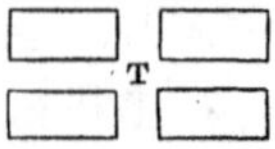

The four stacks are so placed that the threshing-machine can stand either way, thus, borrowing the pencil of Turner, ▭ ▭ T ▭ ▭ T means the threshing-machine, and ▭ the little oblong figures, that do not look in the least like wheat-stacks, *are* nevertheless wheat-stacks. If the wind changes, everything must be changed, and to change everything requires half an hour. But these threshing-machines are curiously interesting. They seem to have almost a vitality of their own. You are never tired of watching them. Sometimes they are worked by steam, sometimes by horses. Steam-power does nearly twice as much in a day as the horse-power, and a steam-engine has to be fed only when it works, while horses must eat whether they work or not. If you are driving across country and see the smoke-stack looming up in the middle of a big field, you leave the road and drive into the field. There stands the monster machine, destroying huge haystacks, but giving in return a steady stream of fine clean wheat, and shuddering all the while with the earnestness of his effort. Two half-bushel measures are arranged in a trough, placed under the stream, and when one is full it can be removed and the other pushed up directly, so that there is no waste. The wheat is at once poured into bags, and is thus made ready for market on the spot. When one group of stacks is disposed of, the engine is driven round to another, till he has ravaged the whole country, — a most friendly foe. Almost any evening in harvest-time, you can hear from your window his plaintive hum, and you can very easily grow melancholy over it. Well may the good-hearted monster be plaintive, foreseeing that the sweet rich wheat he pours out with such painstaking, is doomed to go to the lower States, be mixed in and adulterated with their inferior wheat, and the product called by the name of Minnesota flour, because of the superiority of Minnesota flour to all other. At least that is what the Minnesota people say. The "lower States" men might sing a different song, but I know that I heard an uninterested New England farmer, and a deacon too, say, the other day, that since he had two barrels of Hastings flour, he never wanted any other!

When we have threshed our wheat and burned

our stacks, we plough up our ground for next year's crop, and let it stand till spring. The land is so rich that it scarcely needs manure. It is put on more to get it out of the way than to enrich the land. Little live stock has hitherto been kept, but the farmers are beginning to increase it.

The wild hay-crop is in some parts of Minnesota of the best quality. The prairie grass looks coarse and rank, but is, I believe, universally acknowledged to be the best of all to fatten stock and produce milk. Hungarian grass is sowed a good deal, and Timothy is now getting to be somewhat common. With Hungarian, the land has to be ploughed and sown every year. It will mature in sixty days, and yields two or three tons to the acre. Tame grasses have not generally been very successful.

Minnesota is a good State for sheep. It is high and dry, and the sheep are seldom troubled with foot-rot, while the cold weather gives good fleeces, as I have the best of reasons for knowing. Flocks of five hundred sheep are not uncommon. Some farmers own a thousand.

Now, suppose we reckon up our gains. An

acre of wheat yields on an average about twenty-two bushels. The market price for this ranges from a dollar to a dollar and eighty cents a bushel. With the return of peace the average price has diminished. An acre of oats gives forty bushels, at forty cents a bushel. An acre of corn gives — but the Minnesota farmer is a little sensitive on the subject of corn. "It is not a brag crop," he says, and if a Western man will admit even so much as that any one Western product is not a proper subject of "brag," let us by all means make the most of it. It is quite common in Minnesota to leave the corn in the field till winter, and then haul it in on sleds. We do not top the stalks as in Massachusetts, but cut up corn and all as soon as it is ripe, and leave it in large shocks, and when convenient husk it in the field. In no way will corn keep better than in these shocks, when they are well put up. In Illinois, where they have hundreds of acres of corn, farmers are husking all winter. We feed corn to sheep without being husked at all, and we count it the best of all feed. So do the sheep. They eagerly pick out the ears of corn, and eat them first.

When that is gone, they apply themselves to the stalk, and make clean work of it. There is not a shred of waste.

Three pounds of wool a head is a low average for sheep. The market price may be forty-five cents a pound.

Now for the outsets and offsets which must not be lost sight of. We plant our corn; and just as the blade begins to show itself in rows, the cut-worms begin their harvesting with such success that they leave us scarcely one third. Some of our neighbors lose their corn entirely. Another neighbor who planted a week earlier than we gets a good crop. So then we have lost our corn, but we have learned a lesson, — that early planting is likely to insure a good crop, because the cut-worm is an epicure, and likes his corn tender, ceasing to relish it beyond a certain stage of growth. The dainty little fellows dig down to the kernel and take out the chit. You can see them crawling on the ground, six at work on one kernel. This is a big story I know, but that is why I tell it. You do not suppose I am going half across the continent for the sake of saying that several worms are sometimes found in one hill. Not at all! Six tugging at one kernel, or no story!

Corn is also destroyed by squirrels or striped gophers. If not closely watched, they sometimes make havoc of whole fields, and are a worse pest than the worms, which usually take the corn at the surface of the ground. They have this advantage over the worms, that they are very pretty.

Sometimes we have a dry spring, and the wheat will lie in the ground two or three weeks before sprouting. Then the crop is backward and liable to various ills, and will perhaps yield but six bushels to the acre, instead of the average yield of twenty bushels. To cut and stack wheat costs somewhat more than two dollars an acre; to thresh it, nearly three dollars. The threshers cannot always be had when they are wanted. A company of them, I think it is called a gang, go about from farm to farm, and a combination of untoward and uncommon circumstances, among which I should place first the scarcity of labor, may cause that your wheat is not threshed till the price has declined from eight to twenty-five cents on the bushel.

When our oats are at their best, a storm beats them down, so that of our expected forty bushels we get barely twenty-five.

Then an untimely frost nips the tomatoes before they are ripe, and cuts off the supply of sweet-corn prematurely.

Then we hear that eggs are forty cents a dozen, and, lured into dreams of wealth, we carry all our eggs to market, sell them for fifteen cents a dozen, and come home. Our hens get wind of it, are justly indignant at being turned into merchandise, and for several weeks refuse to lay any more eggs.

Then the Indians threaten to scalp us, and we unyoke our oxen, unharness our horses, and run for the nearest fort, — which is inconvenient.

Then the ducks all jump into the cistern, and are drowned.

Then we arrange to burn our stubble preparatory to ploughing. The Irishman first ploughs six furrows around the wheat-stacks to protect them; but the stubble is dry and the wind is high, and the flame leaps across the too narrow barrier, and consumes the whole summer's crop. But it is a very pleasant and social sight, on a warm night, to see the horizon lit up in all directions by the fires of the blazing straw-stacks. Wheat does not burn so well as straw, and there are other reasons why the spectacle is a less agreeable one.

But the worst thing about Minnesota is, that it is fifteen hundred miles from Boston!

CHAPTER IV.

Fruit Crop of Minnesota compared with the Snakes of Ireland. — Plumming. — Going to Mill. — Perambulating Ruins in Minnesota. — Advantages of Ruins. — Moral and Æsthetic. — Vermilion Falls. — County Fair. — Metaphysical and Agricultural Uses of a County Fair. — Pilgrims' Progress to a County Fair. — Norsemen and Celts. — Leander on the Mississippi Bottom-lands. — Steamboats cutting across Lots. — Spirited Pursuit of a County Fair. — Getting up Stairs. — The Pursuit successful. — Exhaustive Account of the Fair. — Comparison of Eastern and Western Cattle-Shows. — The Mounds afar. — The River-Ghost. — Agassiz receiving a Call. — The Mounds at hand. — A Romance spoiled. — Philosophic Explanation of the Mounds.

BUT we have been so long hard at work on our farm, that we have surely earned a holiday. We will go a plumming, and the fame of our plums shall resound afar. It is amusing to put Minnesoteans to a cross-examination on the fruit-crops. Apples? O yes! Certainly. There is no reason why she should not have as fine a crop of apples as the East or the South. Still, one cannot help noticing that, however large may be her potential fruit crop, the apples that you actually see come from the lower States. And it must be admitted that the fruit of Minnesota is at least a little coy. It will not unsought be won.

This is a general fact, but there is one illustrious exception, for Minnesota is prodigal of plums. Wild in the woods, like berries, the great, beautiful red globes hang on the trees in tempting abundance, — almost as luscious as their cultivated kin-folk. Out we go in the pleasant afternoon of the Indian summer, strolling through the brown, sunshiny fields, crisp and warm to the feet, — aromatic with the essence of the thousand flowers which the summer has distilled; wandering along the steep banks of the blue rushing river, roaring over his rocks, and whirling with many an eddy and many a soft ripple round his green little islands; winding in single file along the narrow path through the copse at the foot of the hill, on whose southern slope the mingled shade and sunshine of oak groves flicker softly around a pleasant home. The copse is aglow now with splendid colors, and its burnished leaves shine ruddy and dazzling in the sun. But its saucy fingers play witch-work with straying garments, and twitch at Jamie's curls most teasingly, as his bright little head goes bobbing along the path before me, just on a level with the shrubs, and the spring of his swift feet is as evasive and as fascinating as heat-lightning. Now the sheltering woods enclose us, and we part the brilliant boughs above our bending heads, and now we come to green open spaces, and the trees droop before us, heavy laden with their pulpy fruit. Carelessly and quickly we strip it from them by handfuls; never mind if a few are crushed or lost, — there are bushels more than the most provident house-mother can ever use, let her fashion them never so cunningly. Plum preserves, plum jellies, plum pickles, plum butter, — so the female Minnesotean tricks out her solitary drupe in "troublesome," but most toothsome "disguises." And so the male Minnesotean brings himself to believe and proclaim that Minnesota is a great fruit State!

Or, if you prefer it, we will take our wheat and drive to mill. Bring up the big farm-wagon, with its span of strong horses; for we are in the country of magnificent distances, and must have ample room and verge enough. Lay in the bags transversely, leaving space for the seats, — though it is no uncommon thing to meet men, and women too, driving teams with no other seats than their piled-up bags of wheat. We ford the river, creeping cautiously down one steep bank, and struggling up the other. The water comes over the hub of the wheel, but the wagon is an ark of safety, and if Robbie must needs give his tail a smart flourish just in the deepest part of the stream, and so administer to the whole party an unwelcome shower-bath, why, we do not mind it, but plod on, jolting and sidling, yet never sidling over, — up hill and down, across the rough breaking, across the grass-matted prairie, twisting and turning through the woods, along roads sometimes firm and smooth, and sometimes given to ruts and gullies; and sometimes we crash through the low brushwood without any road at all, — sidling and uncertain still, but never sidling over, till we come out at last upon a ruined city. Yes, Minnesota, young as she is, has already set up her antiquities. Of insatiate ambition, she is not content to emulate Boston with her Saint Paul, but she must have her Nineveh too, — a city that stood at the parting of the ways, and somehow went down instead of up, till now it is but the forlorn simulacrum of a city that never is, and never to be blest. Yet it has a charming site. I stand at the back door of one of her deserted houses, and far down at my feet the Mississippi rolls brightly between its gayly bedecked banks, and the steamers steam slowly up, and the land stretches back green and level, high and airy from the river, and I think no city under the sun could have a more sightly home. Yet I am glad, too, that the city has dissolved away. Under the levelling influence of trade, I fear the wild bright tangle of these precipitous shores would have been tamed down into prosy landings, and deformed with ugly warehouses, and profaned with foul-mouthed men swearing at their patient horses. As it is, we have this brilliant repose. No rude humanity disfigures the grace of nature. Perhaps, too, it is well we should sometimes learn that man proposes, but God disposes. Doubtless, many castles in the air hung gorgeous above this metropolis that was to be, and when it failed and fell, they too crumbled into dust, and great was the fall thereof. I am glad for no man's sorrow, but we need to learn that the race is not always to the swift, nor the battle to the strong. Even Western energy cannot do all things; even Yankee enterprise sometimes fails. And so for all hopes and plans and efforts this city has played a losing game, and is gradually walking off house by house to swell the ranks of a happier sister, who enlarges her borders on the ruins of her unfortunate neighbor. To-day, as we drive by, the big hotel is rattling down, board and plank and joist and beam, preparatory to migration and transmigration. Grass is growing in the broad, level streets, that knew desolation almost before they had learned population. But from the cupola of a barn that has not yet set out on its travels we see a broad and beautiful expanse of country, with blue hills rising far off, like the beloved hills of home, hopelessly far! Through the clear air we catch here our first glimpse of St. Paul, thirty miles away. It nestles among the hills, a shimmering cloud-city, faint but fair, the central city of the universe to our provincial eyes.

Then we drive again through the oak openings, low woods all aflame with the declining sun, and always we seem to be riding on high table-land, above all the rest of the country, and often flat and smooth like a floor. On such a bit of plateau, we leave our horses under the trees, and pick our way cautiously down the steep rocky bank of the Vermilion River. Stones and shrubs aid our tortuous descent, and we stand at length deep down amid the swirl and sweep and roar of falls, that would make the fortune of an Eastern river. The stream that we forded just now, that murmured along afterwards by our side, busy, gentle, and unassuming, here puts on another guise, and comes dashing over the cliffs with a fury of energy. The river is low, and there are numberless little terraces, curves, and hollows, which fashion each a little cascade of his own. The rocky cliff juts out in the centre, breaking the stream apart, and shaping itself into the likeness of a huge sounding-board; and a royal sounding-board it is, echoing the voice of many waters, from the deafening roar of the main overflow to the soft tinkle of silver drops trickling over the green moss and the bare, brown cliff, or the modest purl of a wavelet stealing into some quiet pool among the rocks. The sun shines brightly among the swaying boughs far overhead, but down among the surges and foam we stand in the twilight of the shadows. Little sprays of verdure, all cool and dewy with the constant moisture, swing down from the crevices of the rocks, delicate wild-flowers nestle in sheltered nooks, and little caves open black and beckoning under the overhanging bank, but they are too small for human feet to tempt. Somewhat sobered by its swift descent, the river rolls through a deep gorge, enamelled with trees and vines and numberless nameless forest growths, — and never heeds that its romantic beauty has been utilized by human hands, — that, disdainful of its untamed grace, but deeply conscious of its motive power, a huge flouring-mill springs up plumb with its sharpest precipice, — eighty-eight feet of brick and stone and glass, — and mingles its ceaseless whirr with the music of the falling waters.

Or instead of wandering about aimlessly among the woods and waters, perhaps it would be more appropriate to our agricultural pursuits to go to the County Fair at Prescott. It will be edifying, doubtless, to compare our own farm products with those of our neighbors. We shall be glad also, to see a Minnesota Fair as against the background of a Massachusetts Cattle-show, and I especially have a great desire to see a Minnesota crowd. I want to see the faces and hear the voices, the ways and walks and talks of Western farmers, male and female, and see whether there is really engendered of latitude and longitude any difference in the same stock. Characteristics come out so strongly and broadly in masses; and to see any large numbers of individuals in this sparsely settled State, one must travel much and tarry long, — individuals I mean who are really individual, who have the stamp and flavor of the soil, unmodified by large association or education. To be sure, Prescott is on the other side of the river, and the other side of the river is Wisconsin; but the river-banks are friendly, and keep up a constant kindly interchange, and we shall likely enough find as many of our own as of our neighbor State men there. Yes, by all means let us go to the County Fair.

The same doughty farm-wagon is our steam-car, horse-car, and family coach, and we climb over its familiar, hospitable sides with ever fresh delight. It has already come to have a prairie look to us. It is airy and roomy and open like the prairie, and like it never full. We drive across country to the river. Here and there we chance upon groups of Norwegian and Irish farmers, coming in from their wilderness farms, a week's journey perhaps, to bring their wheat to market. They travel independently, taking with them their cold meat, potatoes, and bread, and camping wherever hunger or the night overtakes them. With their abundant produce they make heavy draughts on the currency. A merry time they seem to have of it, — sometimes a little too merry. Having exchanged their wheat for currency, they occasionally exchange their currency for something even more worthless; and, with fire in the blood and fight in the fists, merriment is apt to become boisterous, not to say belligerent.

Reaching the river, we descend to the flat-bottomed ferry-boat, and are somehow pulled to the other side; and then we drive along the pleasant bottom-lands, low and level, and heavily timbered, smooth almost as a floor, and intersected by good hard roads, winding in and out among the trees, and seeming stable as the solid earth. Yet, in spring, when the river is high, this very land over which we now pass so securely is six feet under water. The tide mark is plainly to be seen upon the trees, and large logs and prostrate tree-trunks lie still scattered and tilted in rough heaps by the action of the late-retreating water. But the water gives abundant fatness to the soil, and rich grasses spring here far into the autumn, as the sharp-nosed cows divine. They are not usually considered a predatory, or even an enterprising race, but they will swim across the river, Leander-like, for love of these juicy feeding-grounds. Here too, at high tide, the Mississippi straightens out his crooked sides, and we have the somewhat curious fact of steamers taking short cuts through the woods. I wonder what the Naiads and Dryads think the creature is, with its puffs and snorts and unearthly shrieks, its decks and windows and pilot-house, as it comes picking its way among the trees. On blithely through the pleasant grove, till we approach the St. Croix River. Here we find horses feeding and wagons resting in the shade, — prudently left this side the river to save ferriage. It is the outskirts of the Fair Grounds. We are safely conveyed across the second river, sidle up the steep, rocky bank, and are in Prescott. We counted on finding the Fair by following the crowd; but we see no crowd, and, after exploring the street on our own account for a while, we are at length reduced to the humiliation of inquiring the way. The street we are in runs parallel with the river, and travelling is very toilsome. Perhaps the roads have just been mended, for they are deep with gravel and coarse dust, through which we slowly plod back again to find the hill which we are directed to ascend. The town, it seems, is built on another terrace, as high and steep as the one we have already mounted from the river. Ascending, we find ourselves on another of those strange smooth, vast plateaus, which seem as if they were levelled by art, — and so they were, by Divine, not human art. It must be pleasant living on these table-lands. It seems like a great pleasure-ground, as if you were all by yourself "up stairs," a sort of family circle secluded from the outside world. Still, our guiding crowd does not appear. Have we taken the wrong road? It is a pleasant one at any rate; let us try it a little farther. Yes, we are right, for here is the race-course, detected only by initiated eyes, though indeed the whole plain is eminently fitted for a race-course. But where is the crowd? We must have mistaken the day. Here is the high enclosure, here the main entrance; but there is not a man to be seen. We send out to reconnoitre. A man is at length discovered. He is a door-keeper, or book-keeper, or some sort of official, and therefore trustworthy person. This is the day for the Fair, but they never expect to do much the first day. Evidently they will not be disappointed to-day. There is one advantage, however, for we are permitted to enter without fee. It is a highly respectable enclosure, with stalls and booths, and everything arranged in the regular manner. Everything in this instance means eight sheep, one colt, — a tame and beautiful creature, who rests his head against you like a little child, and whom we are loath to leave in his loneliness, — one heifer, one pumpkin, four squashes, and six cabbages. I took the inventory myself. The crowd consisted of ourselves and a bevy of boys, perhaps four, counting in the stragglers. There was also a fruit and candy stand, where, after mature deliberation and discussion, we bought ten cents' worth of candy. For orderliness, I think a Western Fair compares favorably with an Eastern; but for quantity and variety of natural products on exhibition, perhaps the East may be considered as rather bearing away the palm.

We mark well the bulwarks of Prescott, the clean, sunny, open village that keeps house on the third floor, and then we go down the first flight of stairs to the road, and then the second flight, and are on the river, ferrying back again through the still noon, to piece out our day by a visit to the Mounds.

We can see them any time, purple in the hazy air. They are singular isolated hills, rising abruptly from the prairie. One is of a somewhat irregular oblong shape, the other as round apparently as if it had been fashioned with chalk and line. So they look twelve miles off, and we have a mind to examine their pretensions near at hand. The road to the Mounds leads through a valley as curious as they. Certainly, it must at some time have been a river-bed. It is now, lacking only the water. It is a flat valley or ravine, with banks on each side, rising exactly like the present banks of the Mississippi, as high and steep. From the top of these banks the land stretches back level, as from the Mississippi banks. The plain is now filled with oak-trees, and our road lies diagonally across it. As you stand on the floor of that valley, and look up and down along its winding length, and up to the heights on each side, you have no feeling of being in a new State. The grain and growth and energy of the West all fade away from your mind, and you are back again among the unknown geologic ages. O, we know so little of anything! There must have been a river here. Where was it? Whence did it come? Whither did it go? What dried it up? What security have we that the Mississippi will not disappear in the same way, and the Missouri, —

which they say is the true Mississippi, — and the Ohio, and the Hudson, and you, little Merrimack, laurel-crowned among rivers for the songs you sing? And what world was it when this vanished river was young? What people builded on its banks and floated on its waters? O tantalizing footprints of antiquity, Vestiges of Creation! we track you a little way, just a rod or two out among our common roads, and then you fade again into obscurity, and wild, fascinating conjecture. Great Agassiz, mighty Fisherman, Prince of the Powers of the Deep, Kingfisher among men! leave your cold-blooded pets, and tell me the story of this ghostly river. Create again the world through which its bright waters flowed. People again its shores with life, if any life was here. Give outline and color to the pale shades that haunt this voiceless valley, and let us give up our prating of old times and young States, in the presence of this relic of a time that was old or ever a State was born.

Up again the horses climb fiercely almost, out of the silent valley, that just wanders on its way and gives no answer for all our questioning, and we draw near the Mounds. A few white stones on the side of one of them show where our Irish brethren have chosen a burial-place for their dead. One or two homely cottages stand among the Mounds, and only increase the loneliness of these waste places. The Mounds are an example of the bad effect produced by overdoing. One mound would be a mystery. It is as round near as far, and very steep. The top is almost a point. It is like a knob set up on the prairie. At top or bottom there seems to be no irregularity, and by the different color of the grass you tell exactly where the Mound proper begins. If this were the only one, what a romance of past ages could we readily conjure up. Depository of a dead civilization, fortress, beacon-hill, tomb, round tower, — what might not this Mound have been to the wonderful pre-Aztec, pre-historic, pre-every-thing-that-we know-about-ic race which built it? As it is, there are two or three other mounds so palpably Nature's own honest hills, that we must relinquish any human origin to this. Nature twirled it out of her thumb and finger like a top, and it stuck where it fell. The others just dropped flat from her hand, and came down rather sprawling. That is my explanation of the phenomena, and there are the Mounds to confirm it. If you do not choose to accept it, go and look at them, and invent a theory for yourself.

CHAPTER V.

The Result of Feeding, upon Ambition. — Holding our own against the Pretensions of Nature. — A Rhapsody over a Covered Wagon. — Expanding to the Occasion. — The Mississippi in a Decline. — Causes Agricultural and Sentimental. — The Roadside. — Sea-Kings in Minnesota. — A Lakeside Dinner. — Travelling in Beulah. — Grass-growing explained on the true Principles of Poesy. — Doubtful Roads. — Escort in the Air. — Distance lending Enchantment. — Speculation. — Solid Ground. — Uncertain Foundations. — Busy Bees. — The Bridge that carries us safe over. — Hotel in the Transition Era. — Pathetic Discourse to Landlords. — A Surplus of Boys. — Saint Anthony. — Periphrasis of a Water-Cure Establishment. — Saint Anthony's Claims to respect statistically considered. — Brawl between the Mississippi and Mankind. — An Act to amend the Act of Creation. — A Bewildered Saint. — An Appeal to a Saint's Good Sense. — Fulfilment of Prophecy. — Suspension Bridge. — Father Hennepin's Temptation. — Minneapolis. — A Memory.

OUR ambition growing by what it feeds on will be satisfied with no home sights and sounds, however fine. St. Paul shining in the blue distance, the foam of the laughing water breaking in mist beyond, and all the new country lying around this inland city,

— we must see it all. All! a life-time would fail us before we could see all the wonders of this great country of ours. The farther we go, the more wondrous it seems. This Mississippi River of itself is a revelation. Its glory might celebrate a continent. Still, Nature shall not cow us with her marvels. She is mighty here. She pours out her rivers, and piles up her mountains, and deftly fashions her gentle plains; but she knows that man is her king, and cannot be ousted from his possessions. So we will look and linger, and enjoy all we can, — never thinking of the years that have gone into all this "mighty maze," — knowing that one conscious year of intelligent enjoyment is more than a thousand years of unintelligent process. Having thus made all square with our self-respect, we start betimes on a fresh campaign in a travelling tent. This is the zenith of cosey content. This combines the comforts of home and the charms of motion. Hampers, portmanteaus, shawls for cold, parasols for heat, — it is housekeeping on wheels. No slavish subserviency to clocks and watches, but rise, dine, sup, sleep, travel and tarry, hasten and loiter, as you like. Is the Indian summer delicious, the scenery charming? Throw wide open the curtains of your travelling tent, lean back in your luxurious divan, and take it all in. Is the prairie a little tiresome? You have but to dispose yourself for a nap. Is the air stinging? There are plenty of defences against it, and the horses' hoofs will ring all the more merrily upon the hard-trodden roads. O, this is freedom and independence! It is a return to first principles. It is health and happiness. Evil to him who first thought out the steam-car, shrieking, snorting, red-hot, dragging you, will you nill you, through the land of Beulah, and over the Delectable Mountains, with as fierce a haste as through Vanity Fair and the Wilderness.

Now, as we trot cheerily along, we have leisure to take broad surveys. We breathe this heavenly air, we luxuriate in these fields stretching out to meet the far horizon, and our narrow Eastern minds and eyes are rapidly expanding to take them in, — yes, and overleaping them, clamorous for more. Already, I never look south but I see the Gulf waves washing the Louisiana shores. Northward, the deep blue of the Polar sea lies dark behind its glittering icy wastes.

From the east comes the ceaseless whirr of Lowell spindles, and westward rolls the Oregon, and hears many other sounds than his own dashings. Well may we carry ourselves loftily, for our high position is no seeming. We are riding in sight of the whole country; Minnesota is the highest table-land of the continent, they say, and I believe them, for I have been there! California, Massachusetts, South Carolina, do you see us? Elevate your glasses a little, for we are hundreds of feet above you.

All rivers run down from Minnesota, as needs they must if they run at all. In fact, the stanch Mississippi seems to be running away, if reports be true. The oldest inhabitants assert that it is losing ground, and we shall perhaps one day, a few billion years hence, have the spectacle of a spectral, silent river such as we crossed the other day. Well, I am glad I am alive now. and have seen it in its prime; and you, respected posterity, will stand puzzling your brains in turn on its gaunt, unwashed banks, — and see how *you* like it! Meanwhile, we will comfort ourselves with reflecting that the ground which Mississippi loses Minnesota gains. The explanation of its subsidence is, that cultivation softens the soil. The ploughshare tears up the hard, matted roots that have grown and strengthened themselves here time out of mind, and the rain that falls no longer runs off the surface into the streams, but sinks into the mellowed earth. I assent to this plausible theory with my lips, but in my heart I know a reason worth twenty of it. The lordly old river fails because he is faint-hearted. Never, never again shall he go "unvexed to the sea." Late monarch of all this land of lake and mountain and wilderness, he is now reduced to the condition of a broad-shouldered porter, trudging along always with a pack on his back. Pert little villages have stuck themselves down under the shadow of his mightiest mountains, and not one so insignificant but it will fling its sack of wheat or its bundle of boards into the common burden. No wonder the old River-God shrinks from the change. Did the captive kings — "pampered jades of Asia" — wear their most august mien when they drew the chariot of great Tamburlaine? and shall the ancient Mississippi bear himself royally in the service of a thousand petty sovereigns, in slouched hat and dusty coat, not to say shirt-sleeves, — let alone those dishonest Satraps, who put poor wheat into the middle of the bags, and good wheat at the top, and so make the honorable river an accomplice in their petty trickery? O, if the angry water could only suck into his deepest vortex every such sample of man's cupidity, and administer to the guilty one himself a smart sousing every time he tempts him with his knaveries, what an unpopular river the Mississippi would be!

Miles upon miles we travel without coming upon any village, scarcely upon any settlement. There are plenty of lager-beer saloons, — rough structures enough, and not over inviting, but unmistakable on the point of lager-beer, — and we infer, either that there are more people hereabouts than are dreamt of in our philosophy, or that the land supports a very thirsty population. Occasionally we pass a substantial but rude log-house; sometimes a stone cottage, perhaps with no visible windows, — blank to the road, blank east and west, and with a certain squat, uncomely tidiness that indicates Dutch origin. Here is a toy that goes back beyond Holland, a Scandinavian swing, the swing supported in and by a wooden frame, and instead of a rope two long wooden poles, connecting the seat with the pole at the top. "These wooden swings are plenty enough all round," says my friend. "How do you know they are of Scandinavian origin?" Because I saw them in Scandinavia! The Scandinavian is no inconsiderable element in the population of this vicinity, and a valuable and promising element it is. Here again, strangely enough, when we look only for the new, we come suddenly, and, if it did not seem to savor of the sensational, I should say thrillingly, upon the old. Eight hundred years vanish with a word, and we stand face to face with the Vikings. Out of the pioneer's cabin into the pirate's cave. It is the self-same race that swooped down upon England with the raven on their banner and the dragon at their prow. It is the last spent spray of the flood that overwhelmed her. The fierce old Sea-King whom every school-boy knows, — "Thus far shalt thou go and no farther, and here shall thy proud waves be stayed. A king is but a man, and a man is but a worm. Shall a worm assume the powers of the Great God, and think that the elements will obey him?" — this pirate prince lives still in our far-off Western world, but lives with the wisdom of his later rather than the ferocity of his earlier years. The pirate's cave is but a tame and comfortable affair. The pirate himself is an honest, thrifty farmer, who came hither quietly, with some placid womanly face for figure-head of his ship, and with many peaceable families in his company, — yet borne by a power which, with all its seeming and real quietude, would have sent the Great Dragon of his great ancestor to the bottom of the sea, with one puff from its iron throat. Ah well! we were all pirates then, only some were up and some were down. We have all grown graver and wiser since, and Canute is much more worthily employed in breaking wild land in Minnesota, with a span of horses and a good plough, than he was in breaking skulls with his battle-axe eight hundred years ago. The old name is contracted into Knute, and among these new settlements of the old races, Knutes and Knutesons abound. They are but scantily supplied with family names, and Mr. Knute's son is distinguished from his father by the suffix of *son* to the paternal name, — and John's heir is of course Johnson. Here we can see the language going through its processes. It is a leaf of the world's history, taken from the book of the past, and happening all over again under our own eyes. That figure is rather unmanageable, and I respectfully hand it over to the Gentle Reader for what it is worth. But I am not without hope that the theory of "The Stars and the Earth" may yet be found true, so that by travelling far enough we may one day see Adam and Eve trimming apple-trees in the Garden. It would be no stranger than for me to be thus set shaking hands with Canute, Harold, and Hardicanute.

Our Western Scandinavians have given up the vices of their roving ancestors, and have not yet learned our own, so that they are in some respects in a state of touching innocence. They have a most uncivilized horror of debt. A company of them, lately arrived, began their farming-work almost without tools. Their money had been spent in the voyage and the farms. Offers were made to sell ploughs, and other equally necessary implements, on credit, but they refused, choosing to remain their own masters, and work under great disadvantage, rather than become the servant of the lender. I sigh to think how little time it will take to overcome these scruples. In politics, the old Norse instinct heads them straight to freedom. Strangers in the country, strangers to the language, strangers necessarily for the most part to the issues of our politics, — they are almost sure to come up to the polls and vote right, in solid phalanx. One of our public men tells a pleasant story of his own attempt to reach the minds of a group that he saw in his audience at a political gathering. Hale, sturdy men, they stood steadfastly through it all, laughing when others laughed, but with a certain blank look that all his argument, eloquence, and humor, launched directly at them, failed to remove. After exhausting his resources in vain, he inquired at the close of the meeting who they were, and learned that they were Scandinavian new-comers, who had probably not understood one word of what he had been saying. But, noble men, they had adopted their new country, and were determined bravely to "accept the situation."

We dine on the shores of a beautiful lake,

such as one finds dropped into the dells anywhere in Minnesota. A little knoll partly covered with low bushes, and partly "open to sunshine and the birds," is our dais. With the brilliant background of autumn foliage, and the brilliant foreground of blue lake, we cluster on the open slope around our commissary, and feast at a better than Roman banquet, — with the soothing or inspiriting music of the wind in the neighboring tree-tops, and with solid comfort represented in the horses standing by the carriage at the lakeside, and munching their oats, as, unnumbered ages ago, Homeric horses munching white barley and rye stood by their chariots and waited for the bright-throned morning. But the thousand watchfires by the streams of Xanthus were not so beautiful as the soft haze of this Indian summer, warming us to the soul with its delicious glow. And then we resume our journey, winding again picturesquely through the same oak openings, — oak closings I should call them, for they close you in among clumps and groves of trees, about as large as apple-trees, and a little way off looking very much like them, well splashed with scarlet, so that we have a constant sensation of riding through some gentleman's grounds. I suppose they are called openings because there is no entangling undergrowth, but only the bare, hard ground, — sward I could hardly call it, for there is no greensward in Minnesota that I can find, — only little fairy circles and patches of green, soft New England grass, that has sprung up in the wake of civilization. The native sod has no turf. The grass seems to spring up like rye and other grain, with no velvety inviting foundation; but the little flecks of green that appear of themselves wherever the settler plants his foot give hope that the tame grasses will one day subjugate and supplant the wild. So, after all, the poet's fancy is a fact of science. *Quicquid calcaverit, hic rosa fiat!*

"From the meadow your walks have left so sweet
That, whenever a March-wind sighs,
He sets the jewel-print of your feet
In violets blue as your eyes."

"Here," we might say of civilization, — as Œglamour said of his

"drowned love,
Earine! the sweet Earine!
The bright and beautiful Earine!" —

"Here she was wont to go! and here! and here!
Just where those daises, pinks, and violets grow:
The world may find the spring by following her,
For other print her airy steps ne'er left.
Her treading would not bend a blade of grass,
Or shake the downy blow-ball from his stalk!
But like the soft west-wind she shot along,
And where she went the flowers took thickest root,
As she had sowed them with her odorous foot."

For *daisies* and *pinks* and *violets* read *grasses*, and we have a succinct statement of fact, — with a sad exception, for the airy steps of man leave many other prints than these cheering oases, — some for weal, some, alas! for woe.

Very often our road is bordered, and sometimes broken, with gullies, which at home we should be inclined to call dangerous, and convene town-meetings over, and write to the county papers about, and guard with rails by day and lanterns by night. The soil seems to be loose and easily washed away. Sometimes you drive along by the edge of a rugged precipice twenty feet deep, and a precipice that seems to give no sort of reason for its being there. In places the rushing waters have whirled in, and swept away great veins of the road directly across the wheel-track, till you can look straight down, perhaps half a dozen feet; and the traveller just turns out and makes a new track around the hole. I never heard of any accident at these places. Perhaps it is like the story they tell us at the White Mountains, of the woman who thought it was not worth while to go to the expense of putting a curb around the well, as they never lost but two children in it! Certainly, I never saw more haggard-looking roads than some of these in Minnesota.

Nearly all the way to Saint Paul we have an escort of hawks and owls, and other fowl, — no very sentimental troop to be sure, — but a bird is a bird even if it is an owl perching on a bough and staring at you in his stupid owl-fashion. Hawks I have a spite against on principle, remembering the impudence with which they have swooped and soared again before my very eyes, with my own little downy chickens in their fierce jaws, — if jaw that can be called which jaw is none. But these hawks have none of my property on their consciences, and I am free to admire their beauty, grace, and strength. Indeed, they are not only innocent of my chickens, but they are a positive help to the farmer, doing more good than harm. They rarely enter his farm-yard, but they prey upon the squirrels and mice. When a hawk comes near, you will hear the short, sharp whistle of the squirrels in every direction. This is just as they enter their holes and feel themselves safe. But now and then one is a little too late, and finds himself in the condition of the Discontented Squirrel we used to read of in the school-book. Well he may be a Discontented Squirrel, squirming in mid-air in the talons of a hawk. So is kept up that pretty round of internecine warfare, which we all descant upon with so much complacency when we are on the outside of its circle. Occasionally, we scare up immense flocks of blackbirds, which seem to fill the air, and after fluttering awhile settle again on the ground, thick and black as flies, — or they perch on the fence in one long black line till we come up, and off they wheel. Or a group of prairie-chickens sails overhead, or a prairie-lark starts up, hardly yet familiar with the spectacle which has so lately presented itself to the eyes of these wilderness-dwellers. Wild birds of the woods, I wish we could go our ways without disturbing them, — but if we scare the wild birds away, we know the dear little tame sprites that now we sorely miss, sparrows and robins and bluebirds, will follow us and hover around us, and haunt our orchards, — the orchards we are going to plant for them, — and the homely brave little snow-birds will flock to us in winter to pick up the crumbs that fall from our tables.

But rolling prairie and doubtful road and heavy woods have brought us to the busy city. Out from haunt of hawk and blackbird into the thronged and noisy street. There is no easy transition of suburban cottages and comfortable farm-houses; but from the depths of a thirty-mile wilderness we look down upon a stone city, apparently not a quarter of a mile away. As we tarry on the summit of the hill to feast our eyes with the beauty and magnificence of the picture, — the westward hastening sun glorifying even this glorious river, touching the wide, wild, splendid woods to a bewildering radiance, — the city lies below us, a lovely dream in stone, a fairy charm, the beautiful fretwork of the frost which a night has created, which the day shall dissolve. But it is no dream-work now. She had her dream-life, this wilderness city, as many a one knows to his cost. Men went mad, as men do, with the accursed hunger for gold, and great fortunes were made, not by the steady labor of the hands, or the wise work of the brains, but by empty breath of the lips. All the luxuries of old civilization, all the extravagance of newly gained wealth, were brought into this forest, so little was its lesson learned, so eager are we to grasp the shadow without being careful to possess the substance, without which the shadow is not even a specious seeming, but only a vain and vulgar pretence. The bubble sparkled and sailed as long as a bubble may, and then the honest air-currents puffed it, and the honest motes struck it, and there was no longer a brilliant graceful bubble, but there was still a useful drop of water and the solid earth beneath, which is much. So sudden the doom, that costly garnishings, ordered from the East in the height of prosperity, arrived in the depth of adversity, and were reclaimed by the seller as the sole possible form of payment. Women who went to parties luminous with twenty-thousand dollars' worth of diamonds now go to market selling vegetables, and very likely are just as happy with their turnips as they were with their jewels, since a turnip that represents a good thing is far more valuable than a diamond that stands only for a bad thing. Now, there seems to be laid the foundation of a true prosperity. The process is that of natural, gradual, and still remarkable growth. Values are real, and not fictitious. Yet this great Western country is so wonderful, so alluring to the eye, so rich in promise of every good, so strange and vast and uncomprehended, that I do not wonder men's heads were turned.

The Mississippi has somehow given the law of the land. As the river winds along under its steep bank, so our road winds under overhanging cliffs; but the people seem sometimes to have forgotten that their cliffs have not the stability of the Mississippi's, and they have set their houses on the edge, so near, so high, that it makes one dizzy to look up at them. In this easily crumbling soil, it seems to me that their rolling down fifty feet into the road is but a question of time. Occasionally, I see a house set down on a shelf of the river-bank, half-way between the water and the top of the bank. Indeed, the inhabitants seem purposely to dare danger, and, wherever they find a bank, go and build a house on the edge of it. Above our heads here is a beehive, which report says netted to its owner last year two thousand dollars, and the fortunate man doubtless sings among his flowers the pleasant refrain, —

> "And still by me shall hum the bee,
> Forever and forever."

The St. Paul side of the Mississippi is higher than the western bank, and the bridge is consequently a considerable ascent. The piers are of stone, and look solid enough to resist the action of time. There is nothing particularly beautiful about it, but the interlocking and supporting timbers, a little way off, have a delicate, lace-work look, spanning the broad river. The bridge is more than seventeen hundred feet long, and is ninety feet above low water. Once over the bridge, we are in the city, which is largely built of light, soft-colored stone, quarried here. The most marvellous thing about the city is, that it is here. These massive stone piles, that look as if they were built for ages, and would stand flood and fire and earthquake, these ornate façades wrought out with patient skill, this whirl and whirr of human life, springing up in the forest primeval, is a standing wonder of the world, or would be if the world but knew of it. There are wofully dusty streets, and shabby plank side-walks, and shabby shanties; but these are evidently the remnants of early poverty, and the makeshifts of necessity. There is a tendency to truth in building, which looks hopeful for the future. It will not be long before the solid rock will crowd out the *débris*, and the city will shape itself into stately symmetry.

Our hotel arrangements must be supposed to represent a transition stage. We have Brussels carpets, and lace curtains, and linen sheets, and — hatred therewith. Also, the house-builders failed to set their foundations firm, and the house has settled here and there at an alarming rate. We have plenty of waiters and plenty of dishes, but everything is somehow marred in the cooking. I know of a surety that the onions for yesterday's dinner were boiled in the tea-kettle, and the scent of the roses hangs round it still. It is as if everything was well meant and well begun, but blighted in the process. When shall some genius arise in his mailed might, and impress upon landlords the great truth, that three dishes perfect in flavor are more acceptable than a whole octavo volume of *B flats*, — that cleanliness without tapestry or draperies or Brussels is great gain? Why should Minnesota turn away from the delicious repasts of her own farms, to dabble with unskilful hands in greasy foreign messes? Let the old States flounder in old ways if they will, but let the brave new States turn over a new leaf.

By way of comparison, we presently try another hotel. It is an improvement in point of rooms, which are fresh and tidy, and well stocked with a remarkable number and variety of spiders. The mode of attendance is peculiar, indicative of independence and individuality of character. At the entrance two boys appear to take charge of ourselves and our carriage, but the division of labor seems not very distinctly defined; both make love to the carriage, and display a very perfect indifference to ourselves. Boy Number One climbs upon the driver's seat, seizes the reins, and directs boy Number Two to attend to the parcels. Boy Number Two has a noble ambition for horses, and a noble disdain for parcels, and a very pretty skirmish ensues. Between them our parcels receive scant courtesy, — shawls are straggling from carriage to pavement, — travelling-bags shake their plump sides wildly. Edibles and potables are jumbled together as fate wills, and we stand on the sidewalk taking a lively interest in the brisk conflict, and regretfully putting an end to it when forbearance ceases to be a virtue. The same energetic Young American spirit characterizes the service throughout, — or rather those boys seem to be the chief managers. The rooms are destitute of water, and unfortunately of bells also. We prowl about the house, and finally discover a bell-rope in the parlor. Pull and wait, wait and pull. Presently behold a boy! He makes fair promises, but no water comes to our rooms. Another exploration discovers a pitcher of water in a hall below. Probably the boy has again been seized with a spirit of adventure, and is fighting it out somewhere on that line. The pitcher is at once appropriated, but what is a single pitcher among so many?

Then there is no tumbler, mug, or goblet. Our party is resolved into a rotary committee, — a sort of living chain-pump, revolving between the parlor and our rooms, in a constant endeavor to bring up water. Whenever a boy becomes visible to the naked eye, he is caught and collared, and commissioned to bring water. The tumbler boy is encountered after half an hour's absence, and protests he has been diligently occupied all the while in a vain search for tumblers. Boy answering the parlor-bell coolly passes you a well-used goblet, on the parlor-table, for your private delectation. Evidently there has been no such stir-about among the glasses, at least within the memory of these youngest inhabitants; and when comparative order reigns in Warsaw, and you are collected in the parlor in a state of quiescence, a suspicious snickering outside the door, and a furtive eye or two through the cracks, indicate that the enterprising boys, released from their arduous duties, are taking observations on their strange guests.

From St. Paul, the natural order of things takes us to St. Anthony, over broad, high, excellent roads, running through a country well laid out, cultivated, and settled, and bordered by large, comfortable, and often elegant houses enclosed in pleasant gardens. Saint Anthony as a town seems very well adapted to his Saintship, if we may believe the tradition which ascribes to him a chronic dislike of water, a taste for hair-shirt costumes and fighting with devils. A large stone building, with centre and wings, on a sightly eminence facing the river, is the only place that looks like a hotel, and we meditate the propriety of making arrangements for the night, before going farther. To save the trouble of mounting the embankment, we inquire, at a grocery below, if we shall be likely to find accommodations there.

"Wall, Sir," is the reply, with a "knowing" look, "you 'll find plenty of Graham bread and Bloomers!"

Excellent for *entrées*, but not absolutely desirable for the *pièce de résistance;* so we go on, resolving to run for luck in the matter of inns. Shall we laugh at Saint Anthony? Let them laugh that win. While the pen is in my hand, writing this paragraph, comes the morning paper, and says: "The various mills and manufactories at St. Anthony's Falls, Minnesota, produced last year 77,419,548 feet of lumber, valued at $1,885,000; 172,000 barrels of flour, worth $1,661,500; 166,500 yards woollen cloth, valued at $104,000; and pails, tubs, paper, machinery, building materials, furniture, &c., sufficient to carry the aggregate up to $4,348,150. The capital invested amounts to $1,951,000." This I can vouch for; I saw them at it! I saw the logs parting into boards, and the wheat travelling up stairs and down stairs till it lost heart, and fell into flour. I saw the pails whirling themselves smooth, and the slats setting up to be tubs, and vats of pulp smoking hot with the frantic effort to become paper, and hundreds of threads skipping across the floor in transports of delight at the prospect of promotion into cloth. The fact is, Saint Anthony stands on one side of the river, and Minneapolis on the other, and between them both a sorry life they lead the poor old Father of Waters. His back is broken with mills, and his throat is choked with logs, and what with the rocks and the sluices and the splinters, it is as much as he can do to get along at all. Never was there such an over-worked river. It is an unceasing hand-to-hand conflict between man and nature, and man gets the upper hand, at least for a while. Not a current steals through till it has turned its tub, or sawed its board, or spun its piece: and then it creeps away with a sort of shamefaced air, as if it felt itself what it looks, a swash of used-up soap-suds, and not at all the great Mississippi River!

The Falls of Saint Anthony have disappeared in the general *mêlée*, and there is little left but the rush and roar of rapids. The royal astronomer, Alphonso, was it, who thought he could have given the Creator of the universe some important suggestions, if he had been present at the making of it? Our Western friends do not content themselves with a modest, hypothetical suggestion, but, believing that it is never too late to mend, have actually gone to work tinkering up the Mississippi. From what seemed to be the main relic of the fall — of St. Anthony I mean, not of man in general — they have turned away the river in order to bandage up the stone or something, I cannot make out precisely what.

At any rate, there is the bare, brown, wet rock staring out in full view, and workmen fitting some kind of wooden frame-work into the river-bed. This rock is shaped thus:  , and appears to be a broad fence, considerably higher than the heads of the workmen. It looks as if it must have been somehow hewn or blasted into shape, but I am assured that, like Topsy, it only growed. The water has cracked and rent away the rock from year to year. Huge masses of fragments, cleaved off in squares and oblongs and irregular shapes, lie heaped and tilted in every imaginable posture of confusion. Add to this the refuse of the saw-mills, swept along however and wherever a raging current could sweep or set them; piles of logs intertwisted at every possible angle, where the river has lodged them, or lying across half the stream, awaiting their turn at the mills; a constant stream of boards running down the sluices, the never-ceasing snarl of horses and carts, the shouting of men, the whiz of the saws, the whirr of the machinery that from island to island, and from bank to bank, nearly spans the river; and over all and through all, the rage of the mad waters, — and you have a scene of tumult that might make our patron Saint fancy the devils were fighting each other, and had no need that he should lend a hand. If his much-belabored Excellency could leave his deserts, his demons, his caves hollowed in the sand, — could come out of these woods with bell and crutch, to see what manner of place it is that has named itself with his name, — he would doubtless think it but a sorry scene to nourish his saintliness withal. Remembering the wealth and fame and fashion, that he renounced for scourgings and solitude, and all manner of diabolical society, in the cause of holiness, he must be somewhat at a loss to fix upon the especial feature of his life and character which gave its christening to this busy, money-making community, and we can imagine him sighing in half despair, "Who knoweth what is good for man in this life, all the days of his vain life which he spendeth as a shadow? for who can tell a man what shall be after him under the sun?" But I feel quite sure that if the holy man, with the experience of all his heavenly years added to that of his earthly life, would but reflect that here is the best water-power in the known world; that it is the head of navigation on the Mississippi River, and a navigation two thousand miles long; that there is a great country of farms and timber lying behind us; that with our machinery we can convert a whole tree-trunk into boards at one fell swoop, and then, turning the river into a dray-horse, can send them floating down hundreds of miles wherever they are wanted; that a swarm of islands have been dropped into the river on purpose to raise mills on, and that the earth has been stuffed with rock on purpose to build them with, — he would never be so unreasonable as to ask all these people to lay down their tools, and put on a hair-cloth shirt, and dig a hole in the woods, and go and sit in it twenty years. He could not fail, one must suppose, to see that, however adapted such a course might have been to the Egyptian character, it suits not at all with the American genius; and doubtless he would be well content if these workers in wood and woollen but make as good saints as can be fashioned out of the raw material of millers and mechanics, which I take to be quite as good a kind as the Alexandrian variety.

And as I stand here in the midst of the uproar, half daft with the rush and whirl, I can but see how curiously and how completely the promise has been fulfilled to good Saint Anthony. We know how pluckily he defied the demon, when, at his own request, he had been taken back to the cave, whence he had been borne senseless from the conflict. "'Ha! thou arch tempter! didst thou think I had fled? Lo, here I am again, I, Anthony! I challenge all thy malice! I spit on thee! I have strength to combat still!' When he had said these words, the cavern shook, and Satan, rendered furious by his discomfiture, called up his fiends, and said, 'Let us now affright him with all the terrors that can overwhelm the soul of man.' Then hideous sounds were heard; lions, tigers, wolves, dragons, serpents, scorpions, all shapes of horror, 'worse than fancy ever feigned, or fear conceived,' came roaring, howling, hissing, shrieking in his ears; scaring him, stunning him; — but, in the midst of these abominable and appalling shapes and sounds, suddenly there shone from heaven a great light, which fell upon Anthony, and all these terrors vanished at once, and he arose unhurt and strong to endure. And he said, looking up, 'O Lord Jesus Christ! where wert thou in those moments of anguish?' And Christ replied, in a mild and tender voice, 'Anthony, I was here beside thee, and rejoiced to see thee contend and overcome. Be of good heart; for I will make thy name famous through all the world.'"

Minneapolis is just opposite Saint Anthony, — in fact they come so near touching noses, as the children say, across the river, with their mills and machinery, that we are half the time in a maze, and hardly know which is which. Between the two cities is the first suspension bridge ever thrown across the Mississippi, and a work of no small pride, it may well be supposed. One can tolerate a little pride in the structure. It swings in the air as light and graceful as a spider's web, and in its beauty is the hiding of its strength. On the right as we cross is fair Hennepin's Island, in all the glory of its gold and scarlet autumnal robes. With its fine trees, its quiet drives, its shady walks, its brilliant sunshine, it lies like a dream of peace, undisturbed by all the clash and clamor of trade.

If Father Hennepin himself gave it his name, choosing his own monument more durable than brass, he certainly showed good taste, though he did sometimes draw a long bow! Yet I can easily conceive that the adventurous priest became a little bewildered by all the marvels of his journeyings, and, mingling his imagination with his memory, perhaps really thought in his old age that he had traversed the whole length of the Great River, and seen wonderful things. I would not insure myself against a similar result; and as my thoughts have a Northern rather than a Southern tendency, I am not at all confident that I shall not presently write a treatise on the discovery of an open Polar Sea, and the Northwest Passage, founded on my personal observations.

Past the island, across the bridge, and we are in Minneapolis, — a city that seems to have shot ahead of St. Anthony, and already makes no small display of solidity and comeliness in architecture. Four hundred houses, we are told, have been built the past season, and everybody is as busy as if he meant to put up four hundred more. It is the great centre of lumber-trade, they tell us exultantly, and the land round about is the very garden of Minnesota. Better still, I may modestly add, the population of the city and vicinity is largely of New England origin, and therefore we hope not to be ashamed in this same confident boasting.

But I have another thought in Minneapolis.

Some years ago I wrote — perhaps I shall be pardoned for quoting the passage, which has doubtless been long forgotten — of a young woman who bore at school, "in her mean and scanty dress, her thin cheeks, and hard hands, — the marks of poverty and toil. . . . Conscious as she must have been that she served a hard task-master, no word of complaint ever passed her lips. Always cheerful, modest, happy, willing to be pleased, grateful for kindness, and patient of any chance neglect, you might have supposed her entirely insensible to the motives and feelings that influence ordinary girls, were it not for the occasional quiver of the lip, the quick, nervous gesture, the moistened eye, and faltering tone. She left school with disease lurking in her system, slowly and surely undermining the citadel of life; but she kept up her courage. She had no idea of dying till her hour should come, and, as long as she should live, she determined that her living should bring forth fruit. She earned money enough to transport herself to a climate which was pronounced favorable to her health; there, in a wild backwoods, among a rough people, who had forgotten, if they ever knew, the common refinements of life, she opened a school. From her rude home she wrote merry letters, describing her adventures and her circumstances. There was no talk of self-denial, the greatness of sacrifice, the hardship of missionary life. Over all the harsh outline, and the harsher filling in, she threw the veil of her playful fancy, and few heard the mournful undertone that thrilled through the gay, sprightly song. The new scenes and the softer air did not have the desired effect, and a short time since she wrote to a friend: — 'I have moved from a small, quiet school to a large, rollicking, frolicking, fun-loving one. I am happy; I think I ought to be. Every one is kind. But I am quite puzzled, I don't know just what to do. If I am to teach much longer, it would be better for me to return to New England, and go to school awhile. I have earned enough to keep me at school a year or so, and I do believe I am willing to exert myself to the utmost to improve. But, then, this cough increases. It may not be long before it will have an end. If I go to New England, I may spend all the life left me in *acquiring* knowledge, and so lose the opportunity for usefulness that I might have if I remained here. Now the question is, which will bring the largest pile of wood, — the dull axe for six hours, or the sharp one for two?'"

It is over now. Dull axe and sharp axe are alike laid aside, and on the highlands of Minnesota there is a lonely grave.

Two or three letters have come into my hands, which seem to me to illustrate a character of no common strength, purified by no common experience.

"I earnestly desire to write you one more letter, and I am afraid that it will soon be forgery to sign myself A—— B——. Not that I meditate changing my name; but I have a conviction that what you once knew as A—— B—— is gradually slipping away, and an entirely different individual is . . . . assuming her name. . . . . I can see that circumstances have made me what I would not be, and that continued living in Egypt, with its debasing influences, has had its effect on me, in spite of resistance on my part. Once my ignorance of the world, and blind trust in it, was my safety. I called black white, and covered with my charity a multitude of sins. Now, my eyes are open, and is it my fault that I see? It is because I see, and cannot bring myself to the hypocrisy of pretended blindness, that I have feared to write you. I could not write a cheerful, happy letter, simply because it would not be true, and moreover I knew that you would detect the false ring of the metal. Once I wrote a real 'cry-baby affair,' — a home-sick, heart-sick, self-sick effusion; but before I found time to finish it, I remembered of reading somewhere . . . . about hanging upon other people's sympathy until they considered you a sort of mental clog. . . . . So into the fire went that letter. You will never know how many letters I have composed to you in my solitary walks to and from school. . . . . I feel a little desperate now, or I should not dare to tell you that school-teaching is drudgery. It has been growing plainer and plainer to me, until now I am convinced of the fact. I have nothing to say for myself. You will likely think I am not doing my duty. I have said the same thing to myself, and yet I believe I was never more successful in school. People don't know that it is not my joy and delight, and you will not tell them. . . . .

"We never came to an explanation, and at last the news came that he was married one day, and went to war the next. I never heard from him again. . . . .

"After the first day of stupor, the second of pain, and the third of dull headache, I thrust it out, and when it came back to me, at first like a knife-thrust, I held my breath till it passed; then, later, when it came like some unpleasant remembrance, I turned my back upon it, and now the subject gives me very little emotion of any kind. But still, in the face of all, I know of nothing so sweet as human love. I am not one bit afraid that you will sneer at this. I know you will not. I am afraid I should say it again, if the whole world cried, 'For shame!'

"Let it go. There is another world. You will want to know about my health. . . . . I do not know: I am sometimes sick and sometimes well. I have had chills and fever and night sweats this summer, and still a skilful Doctor told me the other day that . . . . there is no need of my dying of consumption. All I want is Minnesota. I had made up my mind to go home and die, but I don't know but it is my duty to make another trial. . . . . I have decided to go to St. Paul. I do not know one person there, and yet I mean to get a situation as teacher. It requires all my courage to take this step."

The step was taken, the situation secured, but health did not come. Another date is: — "St. Paul, May 22. . . . . Dr. —— told me to-day that no earthly power could save me. . . . . He told me to do what pleased me best, for I had not long to live. I have been keeping my courage and my strength up, on ale and oranges, for the last month. I am still in school. The salary is necessary to keep me going, and the excitement is necessary to keep me awake. . . . . I am so tired! This climate of Minnesota is perfectly charming, but Dr. —— says, while it will prolong my life, it *will not cure* me. . . . . If I could afford the expense, I would stay here through July and August, and go to the pine woods, and make one more effort for my life. I would breathe, eat, and drink pine, but it would cost a hundred dollars. I am so much more comfortable since warm weather came (one week since) that I almost disbelieve the Doctor, — especially as another one told me yesterday, that there was hope if I could by any means gain strength before Fall. This climate is superb. . . . . School closes in five weeks. Every one is kind to me, and every one wants me to get well; but I am ashamed that I can excite no better feeling than pity in the hearts of those I meet. I feel as I did when Mr. —— gave me easy questions at school."

Again: — "Minneapolis, October 1. When some people are 'set on their feet' they can keep the balance, and you have the satisfaction of saving a life by one little act of kindness; but others may be set just as firmly, and just as fairly started, and the first thing you know they are down. You have to turn and pick them up until you are tired. I am on my feet at present, and am 'wound up' for the winter; and I do hope that I shall not tumble, but there is no telling. You will be glad to know that I am engaged . . . . in Minneapolis. . . . . My salary is not determined yet. I think they mean to make it depend on the work I do. I have been teaching one month, and have gained in health since I began. So that is encouraging, is it not? I teach everything taught in school but Latin and Greek and music. I have the care of the school one third of the day. If I were only strong enough I could teach drawing, and so help my salary. I was so very miserable last spring, I think I came near death. . . . . Dr. Hunter's Inhalation . . . . was the first thing that seemed to help me. It may possibly cure me. I have gained strength, but no flesh — as yet.

"But I begin the winter with good courage, and very fair health. . . . . Dr. —— says he believes I will die if I stay in Minnesota this winter, but I don't think so.

"I don't read any. Saturdays I rest. I walk round in this glorious air."

And still another note, dated November 23, traced with a feeble pencil: — "I am just rising from what every one called a bed of death. The Doctor said I must die, or rather would die, but I never believed it. They urged willingness, and I was willing, but I prayed, *If* it be thy will, let me live. Five weeks have passed, and I can walk, ride, and eat. I have the *best of care*, — every whim gratified. I sat by an open window this morning. The air rivals June. . . . . I can't write more now. I need nothing."

A few weeks longer she stayed, bravely fighting for life, yet holding herself in readiness to relinquish it. "I am ready when God shall call. It does not trouble me to talk about dying. If my time is to-night, I am ready." One longing, lingering look she had, through the eyes of a beloved kinsman, into the dear family circle from which she had been so long and so widely separated, — and then as she had lived in the world so she left it, with courage, calmness, and decision.

"By foreign hands thy dying eyes were closed,
By foreign hands thy decent limbs composed,
By foreign hands thy humble grave adorned,
By strangers honored, and by strangers mourned!"

Happy hearts will not grudge this little record from the short and simple annals of the poor. I know it is no strange story. A young woman, unsheltered, struggling for life and for a living, — it is a common form of sainthood in our country. A saint? Hardly. We are rather short of saints in this busy community, and she had undoubtedly her faults. A positive nature like hers could hardly be without them, and the mellow growth of ripened years had not softened them away. But if there be indeed some

> "Bright reversion in the sky
> For those who greatly think, or bravely die,"

perhaps our tutelar Saint Anthony will not be the only one to find it. If it be a saintly thing to dwell in deserts and fight with devils, I think she is also not unsaintly who, homeless, friendless, and forlorn, lives in society and works for humanity, fighting all the while the devils of illness and poverty and heart-ache and sore solitude, keeping throughout a good courage, a smiling face, and a cheery voice.

The sunshine lies very bright above her grave. The city's voices do not reach the silent sleeper there. No feet of love will wear a pathway to that distant spot. But in a pleasant land I doubt not she has found warm welcome home, and her rest shall be glorious.

CHAPTER VI.

The Pursuit of Sentiment under Difficulties. — Lo! the poor Indian. — Hiawatha rampant. — A Popular Mistake corrected. — Minnehaha. — Shawondasee and Steam-Engines. — Emigrants. — Milking. — Mars cultivating the Drama. — Fort Snelling. — Investigations. — Philologues, embellished with Cuts. — A Glimpse into Eden. — A Lake. — A Dam or not a Dam. — The Argument. — A Dam that may be depended on. — A Dinner ditto. — Valedictory.

HO can travel in the land of the Dacotahs and not hear

> "the Falls of Minnehaha
> Calling to him through the silence"?

We obey the call, and wander on, yet not, like Hiawatha,

> "Through interminable forests,
> Through uninterrupted silence,"

but over well-trodden roads, and past well-tilled farms. Nor can we wholly repress a sense of sadness, a tender regret for what has so utterly passed away. The last place in the world to be sentimental over Indians is Minnesota. In a country where, until lately, a woman might stand frying doughnuts at her kitchen fire, and look up to see a dark, dreadful face in the gathering twilight pressed against the window-pane, watching the process, and receive for her ostensibly hospitable, but really affrighted greeting, only a non-committal grunt, it is just as well not to rhapsodize over the noble savage. When, in addition to this, the noble savage yells out a war-whoop, whips out his tomahawk, and takes off your scalp, it is all over with the poetry of the thing. But while we may not expect that Minnesotians should be affectionate towards Indians, I cannot help saying that the seed of every atrocity which they committed seems to have been planted by our own white Christian hands. Their violence was the result of our injustice. The wrong which they did to us was born of the wrong we did to them. Long-continued, systematic fraud bore bloody fruit. Government agents and traders robbed them of their annuities. Whiskey was carried among them by the agents of the government which forbade its introduction. The meat which government furnished them, or paid for furnishing, was delivered to them in a loathsome condition. Flour was so completely spoiled, that, when the hoops and staves were knocked off, it stood up like a rock, and had to be cut to pieces with hatchets. But why should we go into details? Official investigation revealed a sickening array of facts. By every ingenious and infernal device, by menace and violence when deceit alone was insufficient, the traders managed to stand between the government and the Indians, and clutch at the larger portion of what was intended for the latter. They sought redress in vain. Is it strange that stupid, ignorant, savage men, having complained and appealed to no purpose, seeing themselves always outraged and overborne by force or fraud, inflamed with rum and rage, reckless of fate and fortified by despair, should finally have taken a rough justice into their own brutal hands? or that such justice, so taken, should have been goaded and maddened into revenge, and cruelty, and indiscriminate slaughter?

It may not be possible for the law to take into account the accumulated wrongs which induced the terrible outburst of savage wrath. It may be that the safety of the State required strict legal penalty, regardless of moral desert; but who can doubt that, to the eye of God, the guilt rested most heavily upon those selfish and unprincipled men whose foul deeds aroused the Indian revenge? On them rests the blood of the slain. The Indians, it seems to me, are to be pitied more than they are to be blamed. I pitied them in the very height of their diabolic madness, for it could not fail to be seen that every blow they struck at us would recoil with ten-fold fury on themselves. They are but a handful of unwashed ragamuffins, from whose smoking ruins no Æneas will ever come out to tell where Troy was. But Vengeance belongeth unto God, and whatever may be our theology regarding future retribution, it is true in the present world that the wages of sin is death, — and death not only to the guilty but the guiltless.

If this were an affair of the past alone, it might not be worth while to dwell on it; but recent developments show that the same course towards the Indians is going on. Untaught by disaster, and with no fear of God before their eyes, wicked men are carrying out the same plans of fraud that brought about the massacres of 1862, and that are still springing up in wars and rumors of wars. They care not for the rights of the Indians, nor the safety of the whites, nor the good name of the government. Indifferent to everything but their own pockets, short-sighted and bad-hearted, they are plunging the State into danger and the country into disgrace.

Having said my say about the right and wrong of it, I will confess that the Song of Hiawatha overpowers, with its plaintive, simple melody, the fierce, wild war-whoop of these late times. The day itself is full of tenderness and melancholy, — a still, yellow, smoky day, warm with the lingering loveliness of Summer, yet breathing through all its warmth a prophecy of departure. Such a day as when listless, careless Shawondasee, In the drowsy, dreamy sunshine, In the never-ending Summer, Sent the melons and tobacco, And the grapes in purple clusters.

"From his pipe the smoke ascending
Filled the sky with haze and vapor,
Filled the air with dreamy softness,

> Gave a twinkle to the water,
> Touched the rugged hills with smoothness,
> Brought the tender Indian Summer,
> In the Moon when nights are brightest."

There! I did not mean to quote Hiawatha, but who can help it? When a poet walks before you, how can you choose but follow in his footsteps? Few enough are the scenes in this young land of ours that have received such consecration; but when you do come upon them, you are instantly aware of another spirit in the air. The woods and fields no longer speak their own words, but are vocal with song and ballad and legend. It is long enough since I read Hiawatha, and yet — so strong is the spell of genius — no sooner do I stand among his haunts than the air is full of the noiseless din of vanished generations, and every bush and brake and tree quivers with that legendary life. The present is as if it were not. Progress and improvement and the lumber-trade and free schools, — they are undreamed of as yet, but on the outskirts of the forest forth fares Hiawatha, with his moccasons of magic and the deer across his shoulder. Yonder in the sunshine at the doorway of his wigwam sits the ancient arrow-maker, making arrow-heads of jasper, arrow-heads of chalcedony, arrow-heads of flint and jasper, smoothed and sharpened at the edges, hard and polished, keen and costly; and the bright gleam yonder is no sunshine on the maple-bough, but the arrow-maker's dark-eyed daughter, with her moods of shade and sunshine, feet as rapid as the river, tresses flowing like the water. We see her face peeping from behind the curtain of the wigwam to see the brave young warrior, swift of foot and strong of arm, —

> "Hear the rustling of her garments
> From behind the waving curtain,
> As one sees the Minnehaha
> Gleaming, glancing through the branches,
> As one hears the Laughing Water
> From behind its screen of branches."

There it is again, you see! Hiawatha! Hiawatha! But it does not come to you as quotation, foreign-born poetry. You see it. You feel it. It is your own thought. The breeze sings it, the waters murmur it. The whole air is vital with it. I did not quote Hiawatha. I wrote it myself!

So, in good ghostly company, we dream on. Scuds across the road an unpretending little brook, that looks as if bent on some merry frolic with never a thought of fame; but that little brook in five seconds is going to be the renowned Falls of Minnehaha, and it knows it, and that is why it hurries away so unceremoniously. We do not know it, and jog along leisurely, then turn aside into a grove, loose our tired horses, and loiter down a wood-path, taking in all the sweetness of the woods as we go, and well content to loiter. Suddenly, almost without warning, almost like a discovery of your own, there it is, — Minnehaha, — the very fairy of waterfalls, — a dainty, delicate little maid, dancing over the rocks with exquisite winsome grace. *Perfect* is the word that rises to your lips. The gem has no flaw.

It is surprising how little material Nature needs when she has a mind for feats. The waterfall is the fall of a brook. It is but a flickering, wavering gossamer veil, through which you can discern the brown rock behind. It is not water, but foam, — an airy, tricksy sprite of the skies toying with the clods of the valley, — mocking the old cold cliff that vainly seeks to clasp her in his rough, dripping wet arms. The rock over which the rivulet falls is carved into a hollow, regular semicircle. It does not fall, it springs over from very light-heartedness. It just gives a little gleeful laugh, — there is a flash, a sparkle, — and away it goes! Why, it is precisely as I said when I wrote Hiawatha, and told you that the Falls of Minnehaha

> "Flash and gleam among the oak-trees,
> Laugh and leap into the valley."

I could not give a better description if I should try again. But the frolicking Undine is a mischievous maiden, and, for all her daintiness, will not hesitate to give you a smart rap if you venture upon familiarities. I have a mind to try the tempting shadows where her white feet rest. I pick my way slowly down the rugged steep bank, press up close to her secret haunts, and, presto! the Laughing Water is changed into a shrew and a scold, and gives me such a swift, sudden box on the ear, as fairly takes my breath away. The spray beats, and the wind raves; it is like a violent northeast rain-storm. I am drenched in a moment, and can hardly believe that the mild sun is shining overhead. The rock projects so much that you can very easily walk behind the falls, midway between their top and the river, under a flat, smooth roof, quite across to the other side; but I do not know that the view is at all improved by so doing, — especially as there is no danger in it, for the brook is so shallow one could hardly drown if he should fall in, though I imagine he might be somewhat muddled for a time. Then the happy river trips away through its deep, shadowy gorge, as gayly and as unconcerned as if it had not just made the most beautiful, the most delicate, the most satisfying little spectacle in the world.

Close beside the wilful, graceful Laughing Water, straight through the land of the Dacotahs, graceless, remorseless, runs a railroad, and every melancholy, frustrate ghost will fly in his mile-measuring moccasons from the snort and shriek of the shrill-voiced locomotive. Shawondasee, fat and lazy, will sit and gaze at the fierce-puffing smoke-pipe longer than he did at the maid with yellow tresses, but this will not end in smoke like the maiden. You, wretched Shawondasee, will be the one this time to turn into a dandelion, and be puffed away forever, pipe and all, by this iron-hearted rival. Alas, poor Yorick!

Midway between the white man's steam-car and the Indian's dog-trot come the lumbering emigrant wagons, white-topped and bulky, drawn by oxen, and overflowing with goods and chattels and children. Tables are slung on behind, kettles swing underneath, and occasionally we see them unlimbering and preparing a meal by the roadside, within sound of Minnehaha, and under the shadow of her groves. Weary-looking, hard-working men and women and children, — all children of toil, — Heaven send rest to their tired feet!

We halt our caravansary too, when the mood takes us, or when some solitary farm-house promises well, and send out a foraging party. It generally returns overflowing with milk, not to say honey. Bread and cheese, bowls, dippers, tumblers, spoons, we furnish from our own camp-chest, and under the brilliant canopy of autumn trees lunch gloriously off nectar and ambrosia. If we were criminals fleeing from justice, any competent detective could follow us by our footprints traced in milk. Sometimes a boy whistles up, stops suddenly, stares a moment, and goes on. Sometimes an overgrown pig — well, not to put too fine a point on it, a hog — roots his way out of the woods, comes grunting up to our rendezvous, and is speedily put to ungainly flight. Occasionally a horseman, or a squad of them, ride by in soldiers' garb; but they are on pleasure bent and peace, for they fling us handbills, announcing a theatrical entertainment at Fort Snelling. Entertainment! Well, there is no accounting for tastes. Perhaps, if we should summer it and winter it at Fort Snelling, we too should be reduced to hanging up a curtain, setting out a row of candles on the floor, and strutting our little hour upon the stage, or before it, for entertainment; but in the midst of the lengthened sweetness long drawn out of these golden, hazy holidays, I am ready to adopt Sir Cornewall Lewis's opinion, that this world would be a very tolerable place but for its amusements. No, my soldier-friend, ride on triumphantly in your brave blue coat. I will follow you to Fort Snelling, but not to any counterfeit presentment, — Fort Snelling, the ancient outpost of civilization, set for a defence of pioneer against Indian. It has been the scene of warfare and a place of doom. Now, it is full of peace and grass and sunshine, a corner lot worth having indeed, for the Mississippi comes down on one side and the Minnesota on the other, and between them, just at the angle where they meet, stands the fort, deep in the heart of all this boundless glory of wood and water. The site is a headland, — if that is a correct use of the word, and if not, so much the worse for the word. Any definition of *headland* that excludes Fort Snelling is defective. What I mean is, that the country behind it, leading up to it, is an extensive plateau, narrowing to a point at the junction of the two rivers, and the fort is just on this jumping-off place. The jump into either of the rivers would be a hundred feet, and from a tower built up at the outmost point the view is magnificent indeed. The face of the bluffs that come in from the right looks as if chiselled into a procession of women in all the rotundity of crinoline and rich fur mantles. I do not mention this as an item of the magnificence precisely, but that is what it looks like. Half-way down the Mississippi bank there is a shelf, and on that shelf there is a railroad, and on that railroad a train comes creeping along in and out, slavishly following the river's capricious lead. Another railroad comes in from the right, about a mile away, to meet it, and while we are looking a train moves up on this branch road, discharges its passengers, and then backs down ignominiously. The passengers stand there, little black vertical bugs, stirring uneasily against the light clay background; or perhaps it is the same beautiful white sandstone that lies in banks at our feet, — so soft that we can easily chip and pulverize it, but cannot easily carry it away in any form but sand. And now the main train puffs into view again, crawls on towards the little black bugs, and swallows them all up. Then it steams ahead, slowly feeling its way over the long bridge across the river, — yes, let me give it that credit. Reckless as our Western friends generally seem, that train did look a long while before it leaped. Now it curves and curves and curves cautiously across the river towards us, and now it roars around the point, close at the foot of the tower where we stand, so that, leaning over the balustrade, we can look straight down the throat of the smoke-stack, and now it rumbles out of sight, and at length out of sound, going down to St. Paul; or perhaps it has just come from St. Paul, for the river hereabouts seems not to know its own mind, and whirls about in such a puzzle where to go, that one can hardly tell which is up and which is down; but I remember seeing a railroad laid on the shelf at St. Paul, very much after the fashion of this, and I infer that they are parts of one stupendous whole.

So we are left again to the undisturbed beauty of the river, here calm and clear, picturing in its liquid depths the tranquil sky, the floating cloud, the vivid forests, the numberless shadows of the shore, yonder rapid, rushing, tumultuous, but always so living, so wondrous fair, that the eye is never satisfied with seeing. Heaven be thanked, this loveliness does not vanish away when the feet turn aside. In the galleries of memory they hang, the rare, glowing, glorious pictures, perfect as nature, changeless as art. The shut eye sees them, the rapt heart knows them, — things of beauty and joy forever.

It is not only a river and a prairie country hereabouts, but a lake country. Lake Calhoun, Harriet, Spring Lake, Minnetonka, — we shall have to draw lots to see where to go. Let us lounge quietly on, and perhaps something will turn up. Possibly we may catch the listless, careless Shawondasee in the very act of giving a twinkle to the water. Wherever we see a gleam of blue we will go and look at it. Here comes a stalwart man driving his double team. He looks as if he knew on which side his bread is buttered, and that team besides is a guaranty of sense. So we stop to exchange friendly greetings, and fall into friendly chat. It is a fine farming country about here, he says. There ain't no better.

There are lakes scattered among the farms too, here and there?

Lakes enough anywhere, if you want to see lakes.

Which is the best worth seeing? How is Lake Calhoun, for instance?

Can't be beat! Lake Harriet and Lake Calhoun are close together. He came by 'em this morning. Good road all the way.

We have heard of there being a beaver dam somewhere.

'S one at Lake Calhoun. Two or three more he knows of, but Lake Calhoun's got a good one.

How much of a dam is it? Enough to see, if you had never heard of it?

O Lor, yes! Shoulder high. 'S good a dam as ever you see.

Fine weather we are having this fall.

Fust rate fer bein' on the road. An' we shall get more of it. Always have three or four weeks of this smoky Indian weather.

Do you ever have any trouble in finding lodging when you are travelling across the country?

Not much. No. I stopped with a man last night down in A. The man was at home, but his wife had gone away to her mother's. He put me up though. She came home in the course of the evening, drunk. He was mad enough. Did n't want her to come into the house. He knocked her out of the wagon and blackened her eye, but he let her come in. I don't like to see a woman used that way if she is drunk, an' I scooted for B. to get breakfast.

Did you get anything to eat?

Yes, sour milk and Graham bread. 'S good as I get to home. Better.

Could n't you get tea or coffee ?

None goin' ! But I did n't care much what I had to drink : only wanted something wet.

"Scooted." I wonder where or what that word came from. It is easy to see what it means, but was it made up out of whole cloth or is it some other word in frontier dress ?* That phrase "whole cloth" speaks plainly of the tailor's shop, but — *scooted?* Another strange thing I saw, an advertisement pasted up in St. Anthony : —

"CREAM CANDY CURES COUGH, SURE POP."

To what known tongue does that belong, or is it the native St. Anthonese dialect ?

They tell a story, — I dare say it may be a part of the regular stock in trade, like the steamers that run in a heavy dew, or raise a cloud of dust, or are got off when they are aground by borrowing a pitcher of water from a farmhouse and pouring it on the sand, — but it was new to me, — illustrating the peculiar use of

* I am told that the word "scoot" is quite common in New England, and means about the same as "skedaddle."

words. A pioneer of some sort is roused at midnight by an unwonted noise. At the high window of his cabin he sees the head of a man just ready to climb in. He presents his pistol to the man's face with the brief remark, "You get!" The burglar looks in his eyes a second and replies, "You bet!" then takes to his heels, and the settler goes back to bed. If Laconia has anything more concise than that, let her bring it on. Another phrase amused me, though I believe it is not peculiar to the West. A man who had been to see one of our famous generals was asked what he thought of him. "Well," said he, "I walked all around him and *gawked* at him, and I did n't see 's there was much in him!" Is not there a picture for your mind's eye, Horatio? Full of meaning, full of character too?

Lake Calhoun be it then and the beaver dam, but we must go back to town and take a fresh start. Meanwhile some mischance happens to our harness, and we repair to a gunsmith's to mend it. He is not at home, but his wife receives us hospitably. They are Germans. It is a gem of a place, and would work into a novel finely.

The outside door opens into the front room, which is the gunnery, — if that is the name of it. Guns, pistols, and a great variety of tools stand around or hang against the walls, but in perfect order. A door directly in line with the front door leads into another room of the same size. Two plump, dainty white beds take up pretty much all the space on each side of the door, leaving a passage-way between to the next room, which is the sitting or work room. Both these apartments are well carpeted with ingeniously made mats, and adorned with prints, — brilliant butterflies nicely grouped and glassed and framed, and many little tasteful specimens of feminine handicraft. It is a mere box of a house, but brimful of comfort and neatness and loving care. The good mistress, an attractive little woman, takes a modest pride in exhibiting her pretty things, and we take an honest delight in looking at them. The master presently returns, as neat and smiling as one would expect from such surroundings. They must be two happy people. They look as if they like the same things, and I think of them living there like two bees in a honeysuckle, — foreign bees, alas! for our

American bees seem never able to compass this snug comfort and content.

We are soon set to rights and come out of the honeysuckle, mutually pleased I trust, but I can only vouch for my side of the house. And then we discover Lake Calhoun to be a bright little beauty sparkling among the hills, well skirted with oak-trees, and describing apparently a perfect circle. At least the verge along which we drive sweeps in an unbroken and most beautiful shore line. The road borders on the lake among a grove, or belt of oaks; and sometimes we take the road, and sometimes the lake, with its smooth, hard, pebbly beach. But where and O where is your famous beaver dam? Why, here, this very road we are driving over is the beaver dam. I do not believe it. In the first place it is not a dam, and in the second place it is not a beaver dam. If it is a dam it must dam something. What does it dam? Dams the lake. Don't you see the water over the other side? Once it was all one sheet; till the beavers came and shut up one end with their dam. Well, if this is a beaver dam, we need not have come fifteen hundred miles to look at it. For aught that appears to the contrary, we may have been driving over beaver dams all our lives. The "long causey" at home might just as well hunt out its ancestry and set up for a curiosity. I counted on seeing the beavers cutting down trees, and weaving in the grass, and trowelling down the mud with their tails, and here is nothing but a beaten road, a little higher than the lake, with trees growing out of it, and everything looking staid, conservative, and human, no more as if it were built by beavers than the frog-pond on Boston Common looks as if it were made by frogs. But we are not come all this way to see a beaver dam for nothing, — wherefore

Lake Calhoun is a beautiful sheet of water, not far from St. Paul in Minnesota. It is distinguished for a large and otherwise remarkable beaver dam, shoulder-high, be the same more or less, and however otherwise bounded. This dam is as broad as a road, and on the side farthest from the lake a good deal broader. In fact it seems to have no limitation in that quarter, but subsides gradually into an amphibious meadow, which would become a lake on very slight provocation. The dam is composed of sticks and stones, and the trunks of trees, some of which are still sticking out with the leaves on them. These are about ten thousand years old, and yet growing. For the most part, however, the dam is well plastered with mud, after which operation the beavers hauled on large quantities of alluvium, sifted clouds of dust into the chinks, and sowed the whole with hay-seed imported from Massachusetts. Since beavers work only in the night, we were not able to watch them at their labors, which are now over, as the dam is finished according to contract, and has been delivered and accepted; but we saw several beaver hats which had been left out over night by the workmen, and were still in good repair.

There is a leaf out of a book of travels for you!

Then we go to dinner.

Dinner consists of oysters, — certainly. Minnesota has such a fascinating way with her, that the very oysters in Baltimore Bay cry tenderly across the country, " O whistle, and I 'll come to you, my lad!" You can hear them on a still day by placing a shell close to your ear, or, in lack of an oyster-shell, by reading almost any specimen of marine poetry. And come they do by the can-full, with the dew of the morning still fresh on their youthful brows, — oysters, roast beef, bread and butter, custard pudding, apple-pie, and squash-pie, peaches and cream, and cake and apples. I tell you, lest you might suppose from the milky way we have hitherto followed that we have nothing to eat in Minnesota but bread and milk. Our dining-room is a fine wooded park, a hill oak-crowned and oak-coated, sloping down to the incomparable lake. Straggling wood-paths tempt us on to sunny nooks, and one rude cart-track strays up to a sign-board, which tells us that it is to

"IKA CITY, 8 MILES."

Happy Ika City, if such a sylvan road as this leads to it all the way!

And still the leaves flutter above our heads, and still the lake sparkles before us, — and the soul of sunshine settles into our own souls too, till through the radiant air comes a voice, —

"Scarcely can the ear distinguish
Whether it be sung or spoken."

"Ye shall go out with joy, and be led forth with peace: the mountains and the hills shall break forth before you into singing, and all the trees of the field shall clap their hands."

But we must leave thee, Paradise. Good by, Minnesota, fair land of lake and prairie, of pleasant wood and rolling water. I suppose you are green in summer and white in winter, like the rest of us. I suppose the sky sometimes looks gray and sullen, and the wind howls as savagely as elsewhere. Into your life some rain must fall, some days must be dark and dreary. But to my thought you are always robed in rainbow hues, and steeped in the sunshine of an eternal Indian summer. Old fort, young city, and solitary grave, farewell. Farewell, sad shades of unremembered braves, tribes, and peoples, a voiceless crowd, innumerable, farewell. And you too, little Undine, Laughing Water, is there no note of sadness in all your singing? O men may come and men may go, but you go on forever. Red-skin or pale-face it is all one to you, and if no face at all leans over you, still sunny-hearted you dance on to bee and bird and bending sky and listening wood, yes, and your own sweet will. Laugh on, dance on, Minnehaha!

> "A hundred suns shall stream on thee,
> A thousand moons shall quiver;
> But not by thee my steps shall be
> For ever and for ever."

CHAPTER VII.

Yarrow revisited. — A Display of Philological Erudition. — Egyptian Society. — On the Ohio. — Temptation resisted. — Piloting. — Reliable History of the Invention of Steam. — The Lost Found. — Visit to Mammoth Cave. — Battle Phantoms. — The Dethroned Monarch. — Nashville. — Chit-chat. — Across Country. — Stone River. — Clay-eaters. — A Sign-board. —Train off the Track potentially. — Vagaries of the Country. — Lookout.

DOWN, down again, borrowing the moccasons of magic, — one step across Wisconsin, and one more to Illinois, and — there is sunshine even in Chicago, and hard pavements, and I have a glimpse of stately houses, and I believe I detect vines, and lattice-work, and certainly a flash of bright blue water. Brava! Chicago. Possibly, after all, with a cloudless day and enough of them, like young Abijah, I might see some good thing may be found in thee. Down and down through endless forests, through overgrown corn-fields that seem to have forgotten they are corn-fields, and to imagine they have kept their first estate as prairies, and stretch and swell accordingly; great, fertile — fields you can hardly call them — tracts perhaps, or counties. Really Indiana and Illinois mean to show cause for their existence. I wonder how life goes on these fat lands. Do rich soils give rich souls?

"Everything goes lovely and the goose hangs high," says my friend, who has travelled often in this as in all directions, and knows much. But what he knows is chiefly social and historical lore. It is I who prosecute philological researches, and I will now inform the learned and inquisitive reader of the origin of that occult line, which, I believe, has hitherto baffled investigation. It comes from the South, where the wild geese fly low in dull weather, and high in fair, clear days. *Hangs* is a false word, — a Northern corruption of the negro dialect *yang*, — an onomatopœian word, representing the "far heard clang" of the wild goose. So in literal fine weather, or in that state of prosperity which may be typified by it, we say, "Everything goes lovely and the goose yang's high." I shall beg to send in my name as a candidate for mem bership of the Corresponding Society of the Pickwick Club.

"But — Egypt, — does not Egypt lie hereabout?"

"O no! Egypt is over yonder. Southern Illinois."

"How came it to be called Egypt in the first place? It is a nickname, I suppose."

"From the Egyptian darkness that enshrouds it, doubtless. The popular notion in Egypt is that 'Grammar talk' is exclusively for the use of people who put on airs and wear 'store close.'"

"I suppose putting on 'store close' there is counted all one with putting on airs."

"Exactly. A short time ago a man buried his wife in C—— County. The mother of the friend with whom I was stopping went to their house to assist them, and suggested to the bereaved widower that a clean shirt was a proper preparation for the solemnities of the occasion. 'What!' said the members of the family, 'put on airs at a funeral! Why, if the ole man gits on a clean shart, he won't come home fur a week.' And the *shart* was not put on. One old lady said she would not like to be buried in such a way. 'Hi, ole 'oman,' said the man, 'you may be glad if you get buried at all!'

"The attendants do not follow the body decorously; they go before, behind, and at the side, without any attempt at order. Praying at the grave is also held to be putting on airs. This, however, is only a modification of the silly sentimentality which prompted George Arnold to request or direct that there be no singing or praying at his grave or over his remains. George must have had a keen sense of the worthlessness of his poor clay."

"*De mortuis nil nisi bonum.*"

"'When scoundrels die, let all bemoan 'em.' Not that George was a scoundrel, — only a wishy-washy poet, and when a wishy-washy poet makes such a request, it is well enough to blunt his arrows by telling the world that he is wishy-washy, and let it go at that."

"Egypt is the stronghold of Democracy, is it not?"

"Naturally. There is a clear affinity between dirt and ignorance and Democracy. It is here that Democracy finds in all its tribulations an unfailing source of consolation. The dirtier a man is, the greater his popularity. It is a sign that he is n't 'stuck up.' To be dirty is the prevailing taste."

"I should think they were much like the 'poor whites' of the South."

"They *are* the poor whites of the South come so far North. They have the true poor white contempt for niggers and New-Englanders; the latter being held, if anything, somewhat inferior to the former. You can judge how well grounded is this sentiment of contempt. One of the families I know of 'pails the cow,' waters the 'hoss,' and washes the family linen (which is a somewhat extravagant appellation for the family apparel) in the same bucket! Most of the dwellers thereabouts keep their cutlery by splitting a crack in one of the boards or logs of the cabin, and sticking the knives and forks into it. If anything happens to get misplaced, the inquiry is whether the seeker has looked into the crack.

"A few days ago a neighbor called on my friend's wife. Wheat-bread was on the table.

The agreeable visitor declared her inability to eat it. She said 'it stuffed her up so.' Besides, she did n't think it was fit for white folks, though she expressed no opinion as to its fitness for niggers. Her taste was for corn-bread."

"Corn-bread is an excellent thing to have a taste for."

"And I must say their corn-bread is good. They had a wedding there the other day. The ceremony was unique. After it was over, the clergyman said to the newly married pair, 'that according to the laws of the State of Illinois, he would wish them good luck and shake hands with them.'"

"If golde ruste what shulde yren do?"

"There is rusty gold enough anywhere about. I have heard it given as a good reason for liking the minister's wife, that she dug all the potatoes herself, and then wheeled them into the cellar!

"They tell a story — I don't know how true it is — of a man named Hogg, who went to the Legislature to get his name changed. The Solons were complaisant. What would he like to be called? O anything; he was n't particular. So the legislators very obligingly called him Thing.

"Last Sunday but one, a baby died in the vicinity. True to the prevailing fashion, — ought it not to be called 'policy'? — the family declined to put on clean clothing. Also they went to the funeral barefooted. The next day the baby's sister came down to see a servant of my friend's. She sang a song which ran thus,

'Let the world wag as it will,
I'll be gay an' happy still!'

They say she was gay and happy, if the unearthly row she made indicated a happy condition of mind."

"I suppose the poor thing had been brought up to it, or down to it, all her life."

"O yes. They are pretty much on a level. Men, women, and children chew tobacco and swear. Two little neighbor-children called at my friend's. One of them was four years old, and expectorated a yellowish fluid, which quite alarmed my friend. 'Why,' said she to the elder of the two, 'what is the matter with your little sister that she spits so?'

"'Well,' was the answer, in a sort of indignant tone, 'I s'pose our Lucy kin chaw tobacky if she wants to!'"

But this broad, rich country will one day be rescued from thraldom. Slavery is gone, and all its shoots and suckers will presently die. Art and science and religion will come in to these dreary intellectual wastes, and the dry lands shall be springs of water. This is manifest destiny.

But we have come out of the woods and the corn-fields; we have struck the Ohio River at last, and take steamer at high noon. The day is cloudless, the river coffee-colored and homely to the eye, muddy and unsavory to the taste, — yet a little way off it cannot help shining and sparkling in this brilliant sun. The shores and scenery are utterly unlike those we have so lately left, but they have an interest of their own. For we are sailing down the late dividing line between Slavery and Freedom, and the temptation is very strong to "offer a few remarks," as they say at "evening meeting"; but in consideration of the national fatigue induced by four years' hard fighting and two of reconstructing, I spare the gentle reader.

I will not promise, however, that such praiseworthy self-restraint shall endure to the end. The steamer is large and showy, but comfortable. We sit on the sunny side, and glide placidly down the stream, enjoying the loveliness of the sky, and the gentle, sometimes beautiful, and sometimes rather tame shores none the less for the mental background of Mississippi bluffs they rise against. It is quiet here and soothing, while the great River of the North stimulates and solemnizes. There are, it may be, so many kinds of voices in the world, and none of them is without signification, and none without its own melody. Perhaps we go up into the pilot-house to get uninterrupted views, and to watch out the lingering afternoon. It spreads up the heaven in a blaze of ruddy light. It softens and fades and dies into the twilight, it is gone, and the great, full moon and the splendid stars come out and take their turn, and the river is flooded with silver light. I am so happy to be alive and see it all. The pilot is civil, but silent. One hardly ventures to speak to him lest it should disturb him, and somehow deflect the vessel from its proper course, and send us all to the bottom. Indeed, I am half afraid he does not want us here; but we asked permission, and he gave it graciously. When we go down to supper, however, he invites us to return, — an invitation which gives instant relief, both as indemnity for the past and security for the future. He tells us moreover that his watch will be out before we come back, but the pilot is always glad to have people up there. He is apt to get lonesome. Thank you, friend Pilot, that is just what we wish to know. May be you have put it a little *couleur de rose*, but never mind.

Supper is a momentary interruption, and we are speedily enthroned again in the pilot-house, among the

> "Silent silver lights and darks undreamed of,
> Where I hush and bless myself with silence."

But our pilot number two is of a social turn, and he makes us acquainted with all the river lore, and amuses us with stories of the guerillas and with various narratives and speculations.

"I come pretty near getting catched once," he says. "I was at the landing down at ——. All at once a company of 'em started up, twenty men I should think, and ordered me to land. I told 'em no, that wa'n't a good place for me to land. They said they 'd kill me if I did n't. I told 'em they 'd kill me anyhow if they got me among 'em, and I started. Then they begun to fire. I was up here, and it was warm weather, and the sashes was back, and there was nothing to hinder. Three balls hit the wheel. One cut the bell-rope. I put on all the steam she could bear, an' seemed as if she never went so slow in the world. She just seemed to float. Of course she *was* goin' like a bird, but it takes a good while to get out of twenty-musket-range when you 're once in it, long or short. Now the head of that gang is put up for the Legislature."

"Do you suppose they wanted to capture the boat, or what?"

"Oh! there was thirty-five thousand dollars in her safe, and they knew it. That 's what they were after."

"But why did they come at you? I should think they would have commanded the captain to give up the boat."

"They did n't stand for captain. If they could

kill or capture me, they could get control of the ship fast enough."

"I suppose your office is as important as that of captain."

"Yes, all the lives on board are in the hands of the engineer and me."

"You ought to be trustworthy men."

"Yes, a man that 's going to be a pilot now has to take some pretty solemn oaths,"—and he gives the preliminaries of induction into office, anecdotes of river experience, and illustrations of the strictness with which the river laws and steamer laws are enforced. Then we fall into silence awhile, which he breaks with the remark that it is very pretty weather. So it is. I had not thought of that before. Then he takes his turn at eliciting information.

"You are going far South?"

"As far as Chattanooga."

"Do you live in Chattanooga?"

"No, I live in Massachusetts."

"Ain't you afraid, coming from Massachusetts?"

"No. Why?"

"O, there ain't no reason, only some are."

"Do you think there is any danger to a Northerner travelling South?"

"O, no; there ain't no danger at all, only from some of the roughs down there. But they won't hurt *you.*"

"But did not the guerillas take a boat from this river, only a few weeks ago."

"No, 't wa'n't guerillas. 'T was a piece of revenge. What they wanted was the mail agent. An' they got him. 'T ain't all they 'll get either."

"How came your people to give him up?"

"They would have mobbed the boat if he had not surrendered. But 't was a pretty serious matter, I can tell you. Stopping a guv'ment officer. One man who was in it went up with us, said he did n't expect nothin' less 'n five years in the penitentiary, but he would do it again! — Do you see them ducks on the water. See how they 'll fly when we drive into 'em." And so they do, but not far, for they are used to steamers I suppose, and soon settle down again comfortably.

How smoothly we divide the shining waters that shine in wavering lustres behind us! "How beautiful is night!" The "silent air" is broken at length by our friendly pilot, who says in half-musing tones, as if it might pass for information to us if we chose to consider it such, or, if not, it would serve for his own delectation. "Steam was invented by an old woman from her tea-kettle."

"Was it? I did not know it."

"Yes, and she made her husband have her spinning-wheel turned by it."

"That is where she was right. I must remember that." Another pause.

"Steam 's a great thing anyhow."

"Yes, it does a good deal of the world's work."

"That 's so."

And then it is getting late, and reluctantly we leave our post of observation, the pilot attending us to the cabin door, and inviting us always to come into the pilot-house whenever we are travelling on the river, which we shall be sure to do; but, O Pilot! I never expect to be on the Ohio River again. It is a sad descent from the outside to the inside of a steamer on a moon-lit, star-lit night, and I am incensed at first with a negro woman, who has lost her cat, and is worrying the crew about it. But her voice is sweet, her manner unobtrusive, and her affectionate anxiety so great as to secure sympathy. The servants listen to her patiently and answer her civilly, but mutter to themselves, "Can't bother about cats, much as *I* can do to look after folks." The night passes as it may. It is but ill-sleeping in state-rooms, and we are up again at four watching out the moon and her long train of light on the water. While it is yet early morning the steward comes in with the lost cat, which leaps up into its mistress's lap, amid a general rejoicing. With such fair auspices we disembark, and are borne in chilly omnibuses, through the gray dawn, across the city of Louisville, and take our places in a car that looks suspiciously like the cast-off clothing of some Northern railway. The seats are flat and hard. The blind refuses to stay up, and has to be constantly propped; but the car itself moves easily, and we are borne safely through "Old Kentuck" to the Mammoth Cave. Fortunately we did not go in, but only rode over the top of it, so the gentle reader is spared the stalagmites and stalactites, the fishes without eyes, the fossil remains and the sublime sensations — fossil too — with which perforce he would otherwise have been deluged. Perhaps the statement that we went to Mammoth Cave needs a little modification; but as we stopped at Cave City, which is but about seven miles from the mouth of the cave, and as the cave is known to extend ten miles, and is supposed to reach many more, it may safely be inferred that the railroad runs over a considerable part of it. Indeed, from what is told, I judge Kentucky to be pretty nearly hollow, so completely honey-combed with caves is it represented.

But more thrilling names than any "Cave" are sounding at the little way-stations. Elizabeth Town, Mumfordsville, Bowling Green, — the land is suddenly alive. Was it over this pleasant country, through these beautiful, silent groves, that Bragg and Buell marched and countermarched all those anxious days that seem already to have been a thousand years away? Are these the rich fields to which the Rebel general brought his impoverished army to feed it upon their fatness? And here we get our first glimpse in his native home of the great, uncrowned King Cotton, — a sorry-looking monarch enough. Let us hope he will do better service as a subordinate than he ever did as sovereign. The cotton-fields are not very attractive. They have a scrawny look. The cotton is planted in hills like corn, and not, as I had supposed, sowed broadcast, like wheat. The snow-white blooms unfold but rarely, only a white shell bursting here and there, as if some one had scattered a few pinches of cotton-wool, where I looked for broad fields of whiteness. But there are plenty of black children, little impish half-naked picaninnies, plenty of women in among the cotton, gathering it into large baskets, and a few men with large, coarse sacks tied on like aprons, in which they place the cotton as they pluck it. They are taking life leisurely. They look up from their work and watch us out of sight, and we are in Nashville, wandering through its twilight streets, with a sad sense of

"Power departed, glory gone."

Nashville, the pride of Tennessee, the bright, the beautiful, the gay, — is it imagination, or is it reality that shrouds the light with gloom? I could think the houses dark and damp, the streets not clean nor cheerful. There are few equipages, no riders, little that speaks of the pleasure or content of life. The new Capitol, an imposing marble structure, looks down upon the Cumberland River from a height of one hundred and seventy-five feet, but looks down also upon a country war-shorn of its beauty. The lovely groves, the old oaks, the wooded hills, that made the suburbs of Nashville famous, have disappeared. It is a bare and dreary pasture, rough with earth-works, bristling with forts, whence not long since the bullets came whizzing through the cowed and sullen city.

And I think of that Sunday morning five years ago, when as yet Nashville had not tasted the cup from which she has since drank so deeply and so bitterly, the clear bright winter morning when there came down upon their wild, eager, expectant hearts, filled with dreams of conquest and renown, the heavy tidings, the doom of Donelson. We at the North remember that day well, the rapture of victory, the sorrow of slaughter, the joy of a speedily advancing peace.

"There are glad hearts and sad hearts
By millions to-day,
As over the wires the magical fires
Are flashing the tidings of Donelson's fray; —
Hearts swelling with rapture
For Donelson's capture;
Hearts breaking with aching
For Donelson's slain.
O, whether the glory
Of Cumberland's story,
Or grief for the slaughter
That purpled its water,
In our bosoms should reign,
We leave in its doubt,
And join the wild shout,
The tumultuous hosanna,
That greets our dear banner
From Donelson's ramparts in triumph flung out.

"Some to-morrow for sorrow
Let Donelson claim!
When over the dead the dirges are said;
But to-day shall be vocal with victory's fame.
Hearts thrilling with rapture
For Donelson's capture,
Forgetting that blood like a flood
In its storming was shed.
O, matchless the glory
Of Cumberland's story,
By our cannon rehearsed,
By our bards to be versed,

When Rebellion is dead!
For joy-bells and chorus
The passion comes o'er us,
To ring and to sing
The tidings that bring
The downfall of treason in vision before us."

And their consternation matched our joy. Panic took the place of pride. The frenzy of terror and a wild, reckless flight, not without some mingling of the ridiculous, made havoc in the fair city, and since then it has been trodden under foot by contending armies. The merchants of the land weep and mourn over her, Alas! alas! that great city, that was clothed in fine linen, and purple, and scarlet, and decked with gold, and precious stones, and pearls! The merchandise of fine flour, and wheat, and beasts, and sheep, and horses, and chariots, and slaves, and souls of men, and the fruits that thy soul lusted after, are departed from thee, and all things which were dainty and goodly are departed from thee. For in one hour is she made desolate.

But we do not say, "Thou shalt find them no more at all." We hope better things. Years must pass before the marks of war are obliterated. Houses and bridges may be built again, but a tree takes its own time, and an hour cuts down what centuries alone can restore. But the restoration is begun. Business is looking up. The hotels are filling. Activity has taken the place of stagnation. A native Tennessean who accompanied us, himself lately an officer in the Union army, thinks everything looks peaceable and promising. The October elections, he says, had a very marked effect in toning down the people. They had got to be pretty arrogant and quarrelsome. There was some difficulty almost every day, but there has been scarcely any since.

"Is there individual freedom in Tennessee? Can a loyal man say what he pleases?"

"O yes. There is no danger in saying anything you like in Tennessee. I don't have any trouble. I don't keep talking just for the sake of talking, and irritating men. There is no use in that. It does all harm and no good."

"But you do not disguise, and men do not mistake, your principles?"

"Not at all. Everybody knows where I am.

But what is the use talking? People who are haranguing all the time, and inflaming others, only keep the spot sore, and delay recovery. There are those who want to keep up agitation for their own ends. I just go about my business. That is what is needed. If a man has sense and tact, he will get along well enough, and help society over a hard place."

So far so good. To be sure perfect freedom is not, until a man can speak without molestation, even if he have not sense and tact. But all in good time. We are at least on the road to liberty.

"Have you apprehensions of further war in any case?"

"None at all. The people are tired of war. Everybody has had enough of it. What we want is peace; something settled, so that we shall know what to depend upon. We suffered greatly in the war, but we are rapidly recovering."

May the peace speedily come, and with the new life which must flow into the South when the idea of human rights shall have fairly supplanted the idea of human wrongs, Nashville will rise to a higher beauty and a greater prosperity than she ever saw even in the fevered visions of her short Secession madness.

Leaving Nashville, the saddest sight of all is the ridged field on the outskirts of the city, the colored soldiers' burying-ground, lying on both sides of the track, — rows upon rows of little hillocks close set side by side, some grass-grown, and others newly made, some with a white wooden slab at the head, others marked still by the rough, weather-stained board which was set in the beginning; every little hillock hiding its story, which no man shall ever read, but together spreading an historic page, which the world has already read, and which shall never be forgotten.

From eight in the morning till six in the evening we ride through a country of wild beauty and magnificence. We wind along the base of high mountains, so close to walls of solid rock a hundred feet high, that we can almost touch them from the car-window. Then we creep along an abutment on the mountain's side, that nature first set and art finished, and look down, down, down upon the river rolling below; and sometimes, unable to turn either to the right or the left, we rumble through the very heart of the mountain, in among the gnomes and kobolds. One such tunnel is a mile and a quarter long, and the lamps are lighted as we slowly traverse the dark passage. Our progress, happily, is never rapid. The jolting, rattling cars speak of years or hard usage, perhaps both, and we must make up in care what we lack in carriage. Everywhere we see the footprints of war. Man has indeed marked the earth with ruin. Devastation and desolation are his contribution to the scene whereto Nature has brought her rare beauty, her best uses, her fertility and her sublimity. The Earth is tumultuous with embankments, the fortifications of a night. Fragments of rough palisades, barricades of brush and stones and mingled soil, are straggling in all directions. Dismantled forts crown the hill-top. A stone monument rises by the railroad-side, so impressive in its lonely state, in the midst of all this wreck, that passengers make inquiries about it, and are told that it is a monument to those who fell in the battle of Stone River. We are crossing the battle-field approaching Murfreesboro; and over corn and cotton fields, through the thickets, in the swamps, across the marshes, stretch the contending armies of our country, its defenders and its destroyers. Over this peaceful land, that lies now so silent and so pleasant around us, swayed and surged the blood-red tide of war in fierce ebb and flow, as now this side and now that gained momentary mastery. Every foot of ground has been struggled for to the death. This bright air has been murderous with shot and shell. This railway embankment has been the breastwork of brave men beating back their country's assailants, — a handful stemming and turning the tide of battle. Hence, in confusion and darkness and storm, fled the grand army that had come up from the South exultant, and the curtain fell upon the first act of "the Lost Cause."

Through Middle and Southern Tennessee, and down into Alabama, — sweet, softly flowing names, — lands rich in promise and possibility, but wretched and squalid. We read of privation and suffering; but the book that opens before our eyes tells a tale utterly new and unsuspected. Can one dream of a life so miserable and meagre as that which stagnates here? It is not life, but lifelessness. The station-villages show a huddle of dirty-white frame houses, small, disorderly, mean, set apparently with no attempt at regularity, built with no thought of symmetry or beauty, scarcely one would say of comfort or thrift, — they might be workshops rather than houses. Groups of unkempt, unshorn, unwashed men lounge on the stoops; men and village are dirty-white together.

But this is the better class of houses. By far the larger number on the road, all except those in the villages, are huts, cabins, built perhaps of logs, sometimes of the roughest boards. One shudders to think of human beings living in such houses, and content to live there. Sometimes house and barn and shed are under one roof, the shed in the middle. Oftener no barn appears. The chimneys are rudely built up from the ground and at the end of the house, with stones of various sizes gathered from the pastures, sticks, and bits of boards piled transversely, and daubed with clay. Black and white live side by side, as it is easy to see, for the door-ways are generally filled with gazers, looking even more wretched and squalid than their houses. One door is adusk with swart faces, at varying distances from the ground, and a few feet away another hovel overflows with tow-heads. The whites seem by far the most pitiable. They have a gray, earthy look, as if the Lord God had formed them of the dust of the ground, particularly of Tennessee clay, but had hardly yet breathed into their nostrils the breath of life. The dress of the women is no dress at all, and but a very partial covering. Bare feet, bare legs, lank skirts, moppy hair, is the costume. One would not mind a group or two here and there, but a country peopled by such beings, a country dotted with such dwellings, leaves a hopelessness on the soul. To ride hour after hour past these dreary, despairing habitations, to see swarm after swarm of these pallid, dull faces, — homes with all that makes home desirable faded out, life with all that makes life lovely vanished away, — O the sudden sadness of it! It seems as if in some sort one's country had suffered change. You thought all was prosperity and progress, even if sometimes a little noisy and rude. But here are silence, submission, and degradation.

The only architecture that relieves the eye is the architecture of the war. Scattered along the road at irregular intervals, perhaps to protect the bridges, are block-houses, I believe they are called, built of short logs with the bark still on, set upright and close together, arranged in two or three tiers, the upper ones set in from the lower, and forming broken but regular lines; they look like rustic summer-houses on a large scale, and both in color and form are picturesque and pleasing.

Suddenly we whiz by a sign, — a white-painted board fastened on the top of a high pole, with the words plainly and neatly printed in black,

PLEASE THROW US A PAPER.

We are out of reach almost before I read it, and I have only a few bitterly rebellious newspapers, — we make a point of buying such, — and I will not add fuel, no, not so much as a chip, or a burnt-out lucifer match, to the fire that is consuming this South country; but how I wish I had some friendly, sensible paper, full of news and good-will and sound politics, and a pencil and a spare minute that I might fling a message to some hungry soul! On the whole, which shall we pity most, he who dwells in this moral and social waste and wants to get out of it, or he who lives here content? The last, certainly, for suffering is a sign of life. Please throw us a paper. It is a sign-board indeed, where more is read than was ever written. It shows a face turned in the right direction. It is a faint streak of light in a dark place. I could not see the cottage, if there was one near, to tell whether it showed any marks of a better thought than its mates, but I fancied that request the work of a rebel soldier, — some lad who went into the army and saw the world, and came back again never to be quite the same as before. He will never again wrap himself stolidly in isolation. He has established relations with something beyond his own village, and he will keep open, if interrupted, communication with his new demesne.

But I cannot conceive of a Northern man in any strait having recourse to such a mode of relief. It is not the Northern way of doing things.

I wish the train would run off the track here, — gently, just enough to give us two or three hours of waiting, — so that we could walk back along the roadside, and have a rambling talk with these people. I should like to know how life looks to them. I wonder what they think of social science, and glaciers, and reconstruction, and the origin of species, and sewing-machines, and washing powders. It must have been in some of these dismal door-yards that the Union soldier said to his friend, a little petulantly perhaps, "Miserable, God-forsaken country! It is n't worth fighting for!" And faith replied, "But it is as good a place as any to make a stand for a principle."

Something hereabouts is very crooked, the river, or the country, or the railroad. We dip down into Alabama, then we run up to Tennessee, then a short cut into Georgia, then we scud back to Tennessee, and four times in rapid succession we cross the Tennessee River; but though we change the place, we keep the pain, pain of poverty in its naked repulsiveness, without concealment, without hope, and without shame.

Shell Mound, Hooker, Wauhatchee, — the squalid huts fade out of sight, and the late years come crowding back again. Through the twilight we are passing into the shadows of a great mountain. There is no need to be told its name. It is Lookout.

CHAPTER VIII.

Shady South. — Moppet's Ideas of Things. — A Charleston Irishwoman's Experience and Observation. — New England in Chattanooga. — Hackmanism in Chattanooga. — Mars bearing a Clothes-basket. — Freedmen's Houses. — Intelligent Driver. — Military Ascent of Lookout according to Intelligent Driver. — Civil Ascent of Lookout. — Scenes within Scenes. — Paying off old Scores. — Historic Doubts concerning Mission Ridge. — Impossibility of Storming Lookout. — Storming Lookout. — Ingenious Manner of giving one's self a little Puff. — Doing one's Duty to the Rising Generation. — The School on Mount Lookout. — Reappearance of Mars. — A Bid for Flattery. — Proposal to carry the War into Africa. — The African proving a somewhat Long Road to Travel, but Ending in Africa at last. — Neatness and Charm of Africa. — Revelation to an Ethiop of the Jewel in his Ear. He bears it like a Man. — Reconstruction.

WE stop in the darkness at Chattanooga, and make a pilgrim's progress to the hotel. The Conductor Greatheart goes ahead with a lantern, and all the Feeble-Minds and the Ready-to-Halts and the Turn-Aways flock after him in a dream. A few steps through the darkness take us to the inn, which is entirely dream-dispelling. In the dull half-light of the lantern it seems to be an old-fashioned low wooden house or block of houses. There are innumerable windows and front doors. There is a yard in front with a little summer-house, plats of flowers, and a plank walk leading through it. The interior, like the exterior, is old-fashioned and decent. The warm weather of Minnesota has given place to sharp autumn airs. Evidently the sunny South is a cold country; but there is a comfortable fire in the waiting-room, a comfortable supper in the dining-room, and a long evening to be disposed of; so after supper we sit enjoying the fire, the constant ebb and flow of guests, and the thick-coming fancies and memories of the place. A little black maid hovers about the room constantly. She feeds the stove, opens the doors, answers questions, runs of errands, but chiefly perches on the window-seat and travels around the room with her eyes. My thought follows her. "Moppet, what town is this?"

"This is Chattanooga," smiling and curious, but self-possessed.

"What do people come here for?" Vacancy. "What is there here to see?"

"Th' ain't nothin' extry, only walk roun' an' see the houses and stores."

"You seem to be all alone here among the woods and mountains. Is there any other town or village near."

"There 's Chickamauga. That 's about six miles from this."

"What kind of a place is that?"

"'T ain't so big a place as this."

"Did anything remarkable ever happen there?"

"They had a big fight there. That 's why they call it Chickamauga." (!)

"Do you know who fought?"

"I forget. I believe it was Mr. Sherman. Mr. Hooker too."

"Did he beat?"

"Yes. Well no, not exactly, but he kept on fighting till he did."

"Were you here then?"

"No. This house was a hospital then."

"Who held it? Which army had it for a hospital?"

"It was fust for Rebs. Then the Yankees took

it,"—and Moppet is called from her perch to hold the light for a woman who has lost some money.

We all assist in the search, bowing over the sombre carpet. A two-dollar bill she says she had in her hand. She is sure she had it in her hand. She is an Irishwoman, but with less Irish than Southern accent, travelling from Charleston to Memphis, and is waiting here for the night train. She took off her bonnet and washed her face, and then her money was gone. After a prolonged hunt she suddenly discovers the money in her pocket. Well, she *knew* she had it in her hand, and she was sure she did not want to lose it. It costs to travel now-a-days. It cost her forty-three dollars to go from Charleston to Memphis, besides her victuals. In the joy of her new-found bill she becomes communicative, and tells us she is going there to live with her sister. Her two nephews are travelling with her. A good many are leaving for the West. The cars she came in were crammed.

"What is the cause of it?"

"O, there is nothin' to do in Charleston! Charleston is all broke up and ruined."

"Ruined by the war, do you mean?"

"Yes, 't was an awful war. O, 't was an *awful* war!"

"Did you see much of it yourself?"

"Yes, I was in it all the time. I lost my father and brother in it. My father was in the army and took sick. My brother was killed at the explosion in Fort Sumter."

"Were you ever afraid for yourself?"

"We was afraid of Sherman and Kilpatrick's men. The Rebs said all the time he would n't get in. No, he would n't get in. He would n't get in. And then we heard he was comin'. But they said he would n't get in. But he kept comin' and comin', and we skedaddled."

"Where did you skedaddle to?" using the word as familiarly as if it had been Addison's own.

"We went to Newberry, — my aunt and my cousin and two nephews. My aunt sold her furniture, sold everything. She had beautiful furniture. She brought it from Dublin. But she just tore everything up and sold out."

"How could she sell if there was such a panic? I should not think any one would have been found to buy."

"They were all in a craze about Sherman. They did n't know what they did."

"How did you get away from Charleston?"

"People went any way they could. We had a mule team. We crossed the Saluda River on just boards with chains. Two men stood one side and two the other, and kept us on. The mules would want to drink, and they had to hold on. I was awful scairt. Moonlight nights we would travel, and camp dark ones. Made a heap o' difference whether there was a moon or not. And we could n't get rest nowhere. We 'd just settle down and then 't was 'Sherman is comin'', 'Sherman 'll ruin you,' 'Sherman this, an' Sherman that.' We were goin' up to Greenfield, an' we heard he was there burnin' an' shootin' and enterin' houses an' doin' everything, and so we came back."

"Was he burning at such a rate?"

"O yes, he just burnt everything. Burnt the crops and the garden patches. Jack Han was a rich farmer up there, and they burnt him out entirely. He 's a poor man now."

"Did they burn him any closer than the rest?"

"Why, yes, 't was revenge. He shot a soldier, a Yankee, for stealing a melon in his field, and the soldiers found it out and burnt everything, and set fire to the town."

"Why did n't they catch him and punish him?"

"O, they could n't. He run into the country. They would n't have known it at all, but a colored man saw it and told, — one of his own men. It ruined Jack Han."

"Do you think the colored people have been changed at all by the war?"

"O yes, the colored people in Charleston don't work now. They won't work. They are all lazy and jes' walk roun'. People advertise in the papers for white servants. They won't have colored people. The colored persons is awful sassy in Charleston. They take the inside of the walk of a white person, an' they insult you as quick as they see you, and if you say a word they make faces at you."

"Did you care much yourself which way the war went?"

"I had a disgust for the Yankees at first. I lost my father and brother. Of course we wanted to be governed by our own people. We 've no use for the Yankees."

The hotel is under the charge of a woman, and there is the very womanish trait of having the best room shut up. We are treated to a peep at it, — a well-furnished room with bright carpet, gilt looking-glasses, upholstered chairs, stately and cold, as best rooms have a right to be; but there seems a touch of New England in this exclusiveness, and we are not surprised to learn that the careful, sociable, modest, and motherly woman who seems to be holding the whole house in the hollow of her hand is a Northern woman. Indeed, her speech bewrayeth her, as it does all of us Northerners and Southerners, Yankees, Buckeyes, and Hoosiers. She and her husband sold their farm, and came down here to make their fortune. Does she like? Well, yes, enough to stay another year. It is for her interest to stay, and, like the thrifty woman she is, she means to stay, like or not. But I fancy her carefulness must be sometimes sorely tried by Southern and African unthrift. Yet she speaks well of her servants, the colored girls. They receive three dollars a week, and are faithful and efficient. She has no trouble with them. But evidently Chattanooga is not the "big place" to her that it is to her little dusky handmaiden. "There 's nothin' of it," she says with well-founded disgust. "It 's the war that has made Chattanooga. There 's nothin' of it but a depot and a store and Gov'ment buildings."

"Are there no schools for the children?"

"O yes, my girl goes to a beautiful school, — a boarding-school, half-way up the mountain. It is kept by Mr. Williams. He is the Principal, but there 's others."

"Is he a Southern man?"

"No, he is from Massachusetts. They are all from Massachusetts and New Hampshire. They are all young. It 's a new school, but an excellent one."

I begin to remember reading of a new school established there by some enterprising, benevolent, and far-sighted man, and ask her if this school is not a Northern affair.

"Yes, I believe it is; a Mr. Roberts laid it out."

"Is there a Mr. C. C. Carpenter connected

with it, — a former missionary to the Caribou Islands ?"

"The very same. He and his wife are in it.'

We must look in upon this school, surely, a school hanging on a battle-field half-way up the sky. Below, it seems but an uncanny place, but may be they are nearer Heaven up yonder.

The morning dawns bright and beautiful and cold. Such carriages as we have been able to secure are at the gate, — antique barouches at uncertain stages of preservation, each drawn by two venerable horses, and guided by a discreet driver; with which brilliant equipages our wayward sisters replenish their exhausted treasury at the rate of ten dollars the carriage for a morning's drive. Leaving our rooms, we are accosted in the corridor by a United States soldier, bravely attired in army blue, tall and respectful and fine-looking, black but comely. His mission is anything but martial. Have we any washing we should like to put out? Of course we have. Are travellers ever without it? I wonder if he is a trustworthy launder, — (laundress he cannot be, — why not then launder?) Does he belong to the house? No, but his wife washes for Lieut. —— in yonder room, and he has just brought home the official clothes. A basket confirmatory stands at the designated door, and he goes away grateful, with a bigger bundle than he brought, but faithfully promising to return it punctually before nightfall.

We drive along the bottom of the basin in which Chattanooga stands. The houses of the freedmen are scattered over the plain, — sometimes crammed close together, and sometimes straying out into the fields adventurous and alone. They are comical little shanties, curiously awry, laboriously patched, boards projecting beyond the walls at irregular lengths, broken-backed roofs, not a straight line anywhere, but every variety of shapelessness. They are such houses as very small boys might build in play-hours, pens rather than houses; but they are generally whitewashed, and look far less squalid than the huts we have seen on our journey hither. They embody ambition, improvement, personal effort to better one's condition. You cannot help being amused at their comical and ingenious crookedness, yet there is a little twinge of pathos behind the smile. The women are at work, washing, knitting, and perhaps gossiping, and the children are playing in the common door-yard, — the open pasture.

We have reached the base of Lookout. The mountain faces us, rugged, wooded, steep, abounding in precipices apparently inaccessible. But we follow a winding and safe road. Our driver is a white man, inexhaustibly stupid or insanely cunning. He discovers no interest in anything, never speaks except when he is spoken to, which is an excellent thing in drivers, — but when he is spoken to he travels a Sabbath-day's journey over the barren fields of his mind before he is prepared to make the startling announcement that he "don't know." It would give a spice of romance if we could suppose him an ex-Rebel soldier shamming ignorance to annoy his late foes, but there is nothing to keep such a theory in countenance.

"Driver, what part of the Mountain did our army take when they charged up Lookout?"

Six geographical miles through the desert of Sahara, then, "Jest along here."

"Did they not ascend both sides of the mountain?"

"No. They went in the road."

"Did the whole army march up this road?"

"Yes."

"But the enemy would have planted cannon and swept them all away."

"Had to go in this road. There wa' n't any other way to get up."

Which settles the question, does it not, soldiers of the White Star, men of Ohio, Kentucky, Illinois?

Leaving the plain, the road turns into the woods and bears zigzag up the mountain. Now at the base of steep, sharp cliffs, and now dizzily along their edge, under great forest-trees, gorgeous with the season's splendid hues. For Autumn, departing from the North, flung his mantle of many colors over this Southland, and draped her sorrow with a more than royal magnificence. The brilliant sunshine streams down through the glorious leafage, which gathers all the lustre and transmutes it into an intenser radiance, till the old mountain is aglow, — a very Kohinoor, — a mountain of light. With every turn in the road, with every opening of the trees, comes some fresh view of loveliness or grandeur, — glimpse of silent valley and sparkling river below, of the long line of purple mountains beyond, of calm sky bending blue above. Half-way up, perhaps, we come upon a level space, a sort of plain or plateau, open, but shaded by grand old trees and home-like with little wooden cottages, summer-houses of Southern gentlemen before the war thundered up the mountain-side; and a charming retreat it must have been, loved of bird and breeze and flower and vine, far up above the heat and dust and noise of common life, won to the sweet solitude of the mountain, deep hidden in the melodious silences of nature. Why should men have sought with painful journeyings our far Northern hills, when delightful spots of greenery lay at their own door? But now the trail of the serpent is over it all. Ruined barricades, shattered earthworks, remains of rifle-pits, prostrate tree-trunks, scarred and mutilated trees, mark the mad track of battle. The road becomes more rough, the silence more sacred. There is no speech nor language, — only the voice of the wind in the tree-tops hushed to a gentle sighing, only the low murmur of multitudinous leaves, — the plaintive undertone of nature. The carriage stops, we alight, we follow the sharp turns of a rocky, climbing wood-path, and suddenly in a moment the whole vast sweep of valley and sky is before us. We have gained the summit of Lookout.

Beautiful for situation, the joy of the whole Earth, is Mount Zion.

I shall not soon behold a fairer sight than this; but it is no fair sight that enchains the gaze, and stills the breath, and sends a shiver through the frame. Not the beautiful river far down at our feet, silver bright in silver light, loitering between its bosky banks on its most wilful way, not the broad valley basking in the sun beneath its mountain walls, nor the mountains themselves, shimmering now afar with a warm blue indistinctness, — not one nor all of these could so fix and fill the startled soul, startled with sharp pain and with a sudden rapture.

To me this is the battle-field of the war, scarcely surpassed in the magnitude of its results, never in the romantic interest of its progress. East and west and north and south it stretches, a line of battle eight miles long and twenty-eight hundred feet high! Georgia, Alabama, Tennessee, are all in sight, and all is battle-ground. Off in the southeast is the bloody field of Chickamauga. To the right stretches the long line of wooded hills that form the Mission Ridge, recalling in its name another tragedy in our country's history, a bitter war of races, a story of oppression and violence, the final, forcible uprooting of a whole people from home and country, and their sad and sullen transfer to a far-off, unknown land. But there are golden threads shining through that sombre web. Mission Ridge perpetuates something better than man's inhumanity to man. It tells a story of Christian love and labor for those whom selfishness and greed and tyranny were grinding between the upper and nether millstones. Verily he is a God that judgeth in the earth. It would seem as if grace and pardon were for individuals only. In nature and nations there is no forgiveness, only inexorable law. The lands wrung from helpless, hapless Indians have been desolated with a greater desolation than the Indians ever knew. Men went out from their homes vowing never to return till they had slain at least one victim. And now in the valleys and plains so wickedly won blood toucheth blood, — the blood of their own children. As it was in a measure the whole nation's sin, so it was in equal measure the whole nation's suffering.

On the plain below in front and a little to the right sits Chattanooga, on a point of land formed by a bend in the river. Puny enough she looks, squatting there in presence of all this grandeur and glory of mountain and river, like a child's roughly-handled and well-worn toy village; but she keeps fast hold of her line of roads that strike out in all directions, for she knows that in them lies her strength. The yellow highways twisting and turning across the valley look like the veins in marble. On the left is Lookout Valley. The wayward Tennessee, running hither and thither everywhere before it seriously sets about escaping from its environment, carves out before us the rude outline of a human foot, — a hint which the valley-dwellers took, and called the conformation Moccason Point. Thence in the battle-autumn our batteries belched up a grim salute to Lookout, and Lookout sent down grim rejoinder. Through all this smiling silence it is easy to see this whole plain astir with armed men, — everywhere the terrible glitter of bayonets, the waving of bright banners bravely borne from many a hard-fought field, the drum-beat and bugle-call to battle, the steady tramp of confident hosts marching under one man's eye to the place which one man's voice assigned them. Before him this wide expanse of hill and vale is an illuminated page, ready to his hand, on which he is to write his own and his country's name and fate in letters of living light. How brilliant the names that cluster on that page! — Howard, Hooker, Thomas, Reynolds, Sherman, Sheridan, Grant, — it might seem as if all the names that have endurance in them are gathered there; but as noble a valor as theirs is the valor which has no name, — the courage, the patriotism, the simple, stern sense of duty that could expect no individual renown, yet just the same put all things to the stake.

Standing here one can more readily comprehend the plan of battle than the possibility of its execution. With the enemy posted all along the summit of Missionary Ridge, with batteries and rifle-pits at its base, and wherever batteries and rifle-pits were wanted, how could our soldiers cross the plain, charge up the steep hill-sides strewn with logs and stumps, leap the breastworks, take the rifle-pits, capture the batteries and turn his own guns against the enemy? Yet they did it. There are twenty explanations and illustrations, — the greater difficulty of receiving than of making a charge, the impossibility of sighting guns at a rapidly advancing object, the uncertainty of shot and shell, but they are not sufficient: the only adequate answer is, they did it! Common sense, mathematics, natural history, and mental philosophy all combine to declare such a feat an impossibility, and the sole circumstance in its favor is that it was done.

And this gruff old Lookout proffers a harder problem still. By nature inaccessible, by skill impregnable, by will overcome. Its surly sides present every form of obstacle. It is ridged and rugged, furrowed with ravines, matted with wild undergrowth, bristling with shrubs, broken boughs, and limbs of dead trees forking in every direction, rough with ledges and detached masses of rock, and so steep that it can be ascended only by literal climbing, and sometimes is not to be ascended at all. The crest is a solid limestone palisade fronting the river, and shelving out at the top, far beyond a perpendicular. He must have steady nerves who stands at its edge; but, sitting or lying on the rock, one can peer over into the craggy, descending, sharp-set abyss below. Upon the crest is a huge pile of rocky irregular slabs, the upper one comparatively thin and flat, and spreading out beyond the lower ones, giving an uncertain-looking but sufficiently firm foothold to whoever would command the very highest outlook. Add to these natural defences that the mountain was lined with redoubt and redan, with breastwork and rifle-pit and abatis; and every earthwork and every rifle-pit alive with plunging fire till the whole mountain-wall was a wall of flame. Now then, come up, men of mortal mould, flesh and blood and nerve and sinew, hurl yourselves against this fiery barrier, sweep the mountain clean of rebels and hold it for country and for freedom. They are coming. To the foe on the heights, the glittering hosts on the plain seem but marshalling for holiday review, — but it is work, and not play, they have in hand to-day. They are coming from the East and from the West. No obstacle deters them, no danger daunts them. Across the plain, into the thickets, up the cliffs, over the ledges, marching, rushing, falling, climbing, clutching at root and bough and boulder, breasting the fierce torrent of bullets, they are swarming up the mountain, they are storming Lookout.

It is another Sinai to the dwellers on the plain, — "thunders and lightnings, and a thick cloud upon the mount, and the voice of the trumpet exceeding loud, so that all the people that was in the camp trembled." The cloud upon the mount wraps about the assailants and veils them from the valley-gazers, but the deafening roar of battle thundering out of the cloud tells their way. Up and up they go, into the clouds, beyond the clouds, and now through a rift the bright banners gleam higher and always higher as they hurtle against the foe, driving him before them by the fury of their onset, and hurling him headlong over the dizzy heights down into the jaws of death. Swelling up the eastern slope the tide of victory meets another sea surging up the west, the mingling waves roll on higher and higher through night and darkness, whelming every foe, breaking over every barrier, raging around the mountain's crest till the false flag is swept away forever and forever, and the morning sun rises upon the banner of freedom, waving in triumph and beauty from the peaceful summit of Lookout.

One bright day four years ago, so close upon these hard-fought battles and dearly won victories that our blood had not yet lost the first thrill of their story, there came to me a little missive from Chickamauga, a "trifle from the grateful hearts of the ——th Ohio, — put into the one remaining hand of a brave, maimed comrade for safe carriage to a loyal State." It was a Christmas letter from an unknown soldier, speaking for himself and his men in words that would shame my slender desert were not their warmth evidently borrowed from the generous sympathy of youth, touching all things with its own ardor, rather than from any fire which my weak hand could kindle. Few things, I suppose, are more grateful to a writer, especially to one who is familiar rather with the salt than the sugar of criticism, than the

"Thanks untraced to lips unknown,"

which help him to keep heart with himself,—not always the easiest thing to do under the constant stress of temptation to fall down and worship a "divine despair." But when words of greeting and gratitude come from out the thunder-storm of battle, it confirms one to one's self with a faith that, for the time, is strength. Then duty puts on her sternest face, and will be served by no insincere hands. What avails there is at least real. How can I ever thank you enough, great-hearted friends, for giving me some priceless share in this Titan work of yours? "Did you think," my soldiers said, "as you read of the charge along the crest of Lookout Mountain, that some of your words went in our hearts up the craggy slope to that 'Battle in the Clouds'? Did you know the van of 'iron Hooker's' bayonets wore a fiercer gleam for what you had written? You did not know what friends you were losing, as that shattered, struggling line toiled up to that pestilent summit. . . . . By no means is it probable that any of us shall ever meet you, ... but when you read of other volleys and other charges sweeping down still more of the remaining handful of the ——th Ohio, please remember that *you* lost friends in the carnage of that hour." O friends! some stronger hand than mine shall crown your brows with the laurel so worthily won. I only come, a reverent pilgrim to the shrine where your young blood was spilled. I press with tears the turf you trod. Over me leans the sky that smiled that day upon your living and wept above your dead. Beneath me lies the rock that upbore your feet to the rapturous joy of victory and pillowed your heads in the sore stress of battle sinking to iron sleep. But I know that whether you still walk the familiar earth, or whether high Heaven holds you, the blessings of my heart within me, the thanks which my lips are all too feeble to speak, are but the pale shadow of a nation's gratitude, the faint echo of a people's love.

Slowly, silently descending by stumbling zigzag paths, — shall we visit the Seminary? No! Well, — yes. Our soldiers are but the advance-guard of schools, and teaching is at best a milder form of martyrdom. I know; yet after the uproar of battle and the pæans of victory, a b ab has but a spiritless sound. Never mind. We will do our duty — on Lookout Mountain if nowhere else. Go to, therefore, and let us get up an interest immediately.

A good man of New York, Mr. Christopher R. Robert, — believing with the Reverend Assembly of Divines at Westminster — on whom be peace! — that, the covenant being made with Adam, not only for himself, but for his posterity, all mankind descending from him by ordinary generation, especially the poor whites of the South, sinned in him, and fell with him in his first transgression into an estate of sin and misery, from which they can only be rescued by God's own grace shining upon their heads and into their hearts, — did out of the good pleasure of his benevolent heart enter into contracts, covenants, and plans to concentrate that gracious illumination, and deliver them out of a state of sin and misery. To which end he bought five hundred acres of land on Missionary Ridge, and as much on the side of Lookout Mountain, together with the government buildings on the latter site. A part of these buildings have been changed from hospitals for wounded bodies into hospitals for worse wounded souls, — souls that have been marred by years and generations of slavery, and its camp-followers, ignorance and meanness. Approaching the institution in the rear, it has still a rather barren and barrack look, but in front a park of fine trees gives a charming playground and a lovely outlook. The buildings have been repaired and refitted with neatness and freshness. As it was holiday-time, we could not see the school at work, but the arrangements made for the comfort and convenience of the pupils seemed very satisfactory. The rooms are large, airy, and well open to sunshine. The school was founded especially for the benefit of the poor whites, though they do not avail themselves of it so largely as was hoped. It was used more by the better classes. Indeed, it is difficult to see how the poor whites that swarm at the doors of the hovels along the railroad could ever get into such a place as this unless they are brought in bodily. They do not look as if they could form any conception of a school, of its uses, or even of its existence; and if they could, how should they command the small sum necessary to enter it? Still this school is an entering wedge, whose power for good it would not be easy to over-estimate. It was opened on the 15th of May, 1866, and expects to form a Freshman collegiate class in the autumn of 1867. It has a Preparatory Department, an English and Business Department requiring five years for completing its course, though permitting students to take a partial course, and a Classical Department in which students are fitted for college. Music, drawing, and the modern languages are also taught. The buildings are capable of receiving three hundred pupils. As yet, I believe, they have but about fifty. The enterprise has not been so far pecuniarily successful, and I suppose was not expected to be, considering that the expense of a twenty-weeks session is but one hundred dollars.

Some of the "Rules and Regulations" are interesting, as compared with those of similar institutions at the North. Number One is that "No profane or vulgar language is permitted in the Institutions."

Number Two. The use of tobacco is not allowed in any of the buildings or upon the verandas.

Number Three. No student will be allowed to remain in the Institutions who makes use of intoxicating liquors.

Number Six. Scholars are required to be neatly dressed, and to be punctual and regular in their attendance upon the exercises of the schools.

Boys and girls over twelve years of age are admitted. Several Rebel and Union soldiers have been among the pupils. All the teachers are away for the vacation, but the business manager and the matron, Rev. and Mrs. C. C. Carpenter, late of Caribou Island, are keeping castle, pleasing themselves doubtless with reproducing as far as possible the lost delights of Labrador climate and society by perching on the mountain peaks of Tennessee. As far as one may judge from so very slight a survey, the school is worthy of the confidence and support of the North, and full of promise to the South.

I am just preparing to steal out of my room to take a quiet walk by myself, and get a face-to-face glimpse of Chattanooga, when there is a knock at the door, and there stands my six-foot soldier with his well-filled basket of clean clothes. His promptness surprises me, and my admiration of his promptness gratifies him. "Is it possible your wife has washed and ironed all these clothes to-day?"—for it seems nearly as impracticable a thing as the storming of Lookout.

"Yes, Miss," he says modestly, his whole swart face illuminated with smiles.

"Did she do them all alone?"

"Yes, Miss. I 've got a wife that *is* a wife."

"I should think so. And they are very nicely done too."

"Yes, I told her she must do her prettiest on yours."

Now I do not suppose he did tell her any such thing, there being no reason in the world why he should, but then it was very civil in him to say so. You may not put implicit confidence in everything your flatterers tell you, but it is pleasant to know that people care enough about pleasing you to flatter you. Attempting to pay him, I find I must have a bill changed. He cannot change it, nor the landlady, nor the clerk; so I propose to go out with him into some of the neighboring shops, and then I adjure him to take the money home and give it to his wife with my thanks and respects. He promises me faithfully that he will, only he is not going directly home. It occurs to me, "Why not go and pay her myself? I should like to tell her how highly I think of her work. Do you suppose she would object to my paying her a visit?"

"Indeed, she 'd be very much pleased. Nothing she likes better than to do things for people and have it please them."

"How far away do you live?"

"Not a great ways, — half a mile perhaps, or three quarters."

"You can show me the way so that I can find it without trouble?"

"I've got through my day's work, Miss, and I can go with you myself, just as well as not." So we walk off together amicably, and he says in a low voice, half to himself, "She 'll be mighty proud to have you come and see her."

My companion justifies my instinctive good opinion of him. His manners are gentle, his voice is low and smooth, and his talk intelligent. He tells me that he is a freedman, that he used to live in Georgia, but left his master and followed Mr. Sherman's army, and has never seen his master since. He went first to Atalanta, and then came up to Chattanooga.

"Did your wife come with you?"

"No, she lived with another master and could n't get away. I did n't know not'in' what become of her. Fust I knowed a party of fugitives said she was comin' up on de cars. Soon 's I heard of her, I went and got her."

"Was she freed by the army?"

"No, she runned away from her Mas'r too, and took the boy wid her. But de Rebels got hold of him and carried him back thirteen miles, but he got away from 'em in de night an' run back to his moder. She left everyting, — bed an' beddin', — did n't bring notin' wid her only three dresses. We scraped a bed an' a few tings togeder, and managed to get along."

"How old was the boy?"

"Leben years, Miss."

"He must be a very bright boy."

"Yes, he 's a good boy."

"And I hope you will send him to school and give him a good education."

"Yes, my wife an' me, we 's goin' to give the boy larnin', and then I tell him he must work an' be civil an' well-mannered, an' that 's all that 's nec'ary."

"Do you have regular work yourself?"

"Yes, Miss. I 'se employed on the railroad. I get forty dollars a month. I 'se been a railroad man now two years."

"That is very good wages."

"Yes, but everyting 's very high. I pay ten dollars a month rent, an' it takes about all there is left to live on. I don't get much ahead. Took a heap of money to get started."

"Do the white people trouble you at all here?"

"Well, no. Dey can't do notin' cause dere 's de sogers."

"Do you suppose they would harm you if the soldiers were removed?"

"Good many people roun' here that would be cuttin' up if dey was away."

"'Cutting up,' — how?"

"Well, they 'd be down on us!"

The variations in his pronunciation are I believe his, and not mine. I distinctly remember certain words in which *th* was changed into *d*. Others I remember with the proper sound, and give them so. It may be that his conversation represents a transition state in his education.

The road is getting rather rough and wild, seems indeed to be chiefly railroad, and I fancy we have already gone our three quarters of a mile. He says that we are now pretty near the house, but he seems to be a little absent-minded, and finally stops and says: "I *will* speak of it. Miss, you must excuse me, — I ony jess thought of it, — I ought to have told you, — but I noticed you come away and left your door open."

"Why, so I did. I forgot. However, I don't believe any one will go in."

"No, I don't *believe* they will. Nobody roun'

to see it ony me an' the lady, but I thought I would jess mention it."

Here it occurs to me that I have left my hotel without anybody's knowing where I am, or whither I am going, or that I am gone at all; indeed, on the first two points I have but a slender stock of information myself. I trust this is an honest man. I steal a sidelong glance up into his face, and am shamed out of my momentary distrust. It is radiant with gentleness and honesty and satisfaction and modesty. Let us deviate into politics.

"Do the colored people feel much interest in the question of suffrage?"

"Well, some does and some does n't. They don't say a great deal about it."

"How do you look upon it yourself?"

"Seems like there ain't no hurry about it. I think they better wait till they get more larnin'."

"If they should be allowed to vote how do you think they would vote?"

"Oh!" with a decidedly derisive laugh, "they 'd vote as they thought"; — then as an unnecessary appendix, "Of course they 'd vote wid de Yankees."

Then we turn into something more like a street, and soon he opens for me a gate, saying, "Here 's whar I live." It is a low, broad house, without pretensions to beauty, but sufficiently comfortable. "No, not de big house. Dis whar de lady lives who owns my house." We go past the landlady's house, around into the back yard, and come to his own dwelling. It looks like a shed or porch of the larger house, but is whitewashed and well kept. A part of the yard is hard and clean-swept, and a part is devoted to gardening. The door stands open, leading directly to their living-room, where his wife appears resting from her labors. Our introduction is historical rather than fashionable. She is a young woman, not so prepossessing as her husband, for whom she evidently has a great respect, not to say reverence. She seems like a little girl, almost too bashful to speak, but she has a bright smile, and she presently opens to me, and we speedily get on terms friendly, not to say intimate, discussing her boy, her husband, her skill, and the beauties of Chattanooga. The room is the perfection of neatness. It has a look of being thick-set with household implements and other trumpery, — braided mats among the rest, though of course I make a point of not seeing anything.

When I rise to go, the husband insists on accompanying me to show the way, and as we are leaving the yard he says apologetically, "She ain't a very fancy woman, but she's smart, and you must make the best of it."

Oh! but then do I not wax rhetorical, extolling not only her virtues, but her charms; and it is no fault of mine if he does not go home marvelling at the jewel he has so long possessed all unknown. Indeed, I half fancy he thinks he must somehow have introduced me to the wrong woman, but he does not stint his praises. "She ain't nothin' for company," he says. "She been here now fourteen months and she has n't taken tea out once. She don't go nowhar, only to church."

"Is she a member of the church?"

"Yes, she's been a member of the Methodist church eighteen years."

"Do the colored people here go to church as a general thing?"

"Very much same as 't is wid de whites. Some goes and some does n't."

"Do you think they generally use their freedom? Do they behave well?"

"Some of 'em is industrious and behaves well, and some of 'em is lazy and steals, and is sent to the penitentiary. Dere was one ony little while ago. That 's what disheartens me most of anything. I talk to 'em an' try to make 'em do better."

And then what if I give him some encouraging assurances, and a little friendly suggestion, and just a spice of flattery founded on fact, in return for his civility; and he offers me unlimited service whenever I return to Chattanooga, and we part like Pip and Joe Gargery, "us ever the best of friends," — does it not all come into the general plan of Reconstruction?

CHAPTER IX.

Fame Waiting a Name. — Officers' Car. — Topsy by Night. — Relieving Burnside. — Knoxville. — Comfortable Reflections for a Besieged Town. — Holding on. — Fort Saunders. — Return to Knoxville. — The Dead. — The Living. — New England. — A Plan of Reconstruction. — Pauperism North and South. — Hatred, its Causes and Cures. — Playing off the South and West against each other.

WE rise at midnight to march to the relief of General Burnside in beleaguered Knoxville. Our Household Friend is at hand to speed the parting guest; and as we exchange words, she is for the first time curious in names. "Smith? Smith?" She lingers on the novel sound, as if calling up from the vasty deep of her memory some familiar thought to associate with the strange fact. It is n't the Smith that writes? O no! The Smiths never write. They simply make their mark. She is but half convinced, and affirms dubiously and interrogatively that she has heard of a Smith who writes beautiful pieces! But we know no Smith who can lay claim to such distinction, and, bidding her a grateful good-by, we go out into the starry darkness. Lookout rises grand and gloomy, giving no sign of that awful night which belted his form with fire, when victory thundered from his sides with a thousand tongues of flame, and disaster waved to disaster from the signal torch on his crest.

Comfortable quarters are secured in the "officers' car," which is provided with long sofas, where, for aught I know, many campaigns may have been thought out before they were fought out, during the four years' war. One of these sofas is soon occupied by a young man, an invalid, whom his father is taking home, pale, emaciated, too deathly sick to utter a word. Our medicine-chest is produced, and his failing strength fortified from the brandy-flask, which thus vindicates its right to be. His father watches with restless, painful anxiety his flickering life, in the absorbing fear that it may not outlast the long journey. At one of the small way-stations comes in a little olive-hued girl, with wild, jet-black, unearthly eyes, all alight with a sort of strange mockery and impish laughter. A little creature it is, who should be sleeping soundly in her bed, instead of vending hot coffee through the cars at this time of night. I wonder if it is not this preternatural wakefulness that has struck into her eyes and into her soul, and inspired her to see and scorn the satire of her life. "Running about alone all night, Topsy! Why, you must be a little owl."

"Yes 'm. I 'spect that 's what 's the matter!" is the quick, pert reply, with a flash of the wild eyes, and a saucy toss of the small head.

We rush on through the darkness, over the same road that Burnside took, backing into Knoxville with his face to the foe, and fighting as he went, — over the same road that Sherman marched, and by sheer force of his name and his numbers sent Longstreet flying from Knoxville, with Burnside's cavalry at his heels. In the darkness we fight our battles o'er again. How grandly our soldier met in his mountain fastnesses the exigency of the time! What stress of fate is in the words of the imperturbable

Grant, "I do not know how to impress on you the necessity of holding on to East Tennessee in strong enough terms." And hold on he did, with a grip that neither long siege nor sharp assault could loosen.

To Knoxville, city of the mountains, environed by frowning forts, and forever memorable for that heroic and successful defence. But what with friend and what with foe, Knoxville has had but sorry fortunes. Fire and sword have made wretched work for the mountain town. The necessity and the wantonness of war have alike ravaged here. In the suburbs the axe has turned the forest into a cleared field, and at one end of the city fire has wellnigh made a clean sweep. When a great cause is marching on, I suppose there must be minor irregularities. Indeed, war itself is a monstrous irregularity, and all lesser ones crowd to its banners. If the individual withers a little under the infliction, he can console himself with reflecting that the world is more and more. So when troops are camping in your door-yard, pulling down your neat fences, your fine trees, your pretty shrubbery to boil their coffee with, and boiling it in your kitchen, and sleeping in your bed-rooms, borrowing your knives and forks and napkins and towels with charming frankness and frankly forgetting to return them, it may perhaps salve your wounds to know that your hardware and haberdashery are not going to swell the gains of some ignoble thief, but to furnish creature comforts for the great cause of human freedom and human progress! Besides, our troops were unselfish, and when they had levelled the pal ing of a loyal citizen, would generously offer to share their hard-earned firewood with him!

We go round about Knoxville, telling her towers and marking well her bulwarks. We pass through her lines of defence, still well defined. We see the remnants of the barricades that stretched across her country roads. Line upon line of defence, precept upon precept of resistance, but no point of surrender. Burnside was holding on! Driven from one position, the troops were to fall back to another. And in the final issue they were to withdraw into the city and make every house a fortress. But it did not come to that. Thank Heaven! it never came to that.

We drive out to Fort Saunders, where was met the fierce assault, the last desperate resort of Longstreet's failing force. Fort Saunders, named in honor of the brave young Kentuckian who, in front of the fort, at the front of all danger, received his death-wound, and was borne hence to his midnight burial. We climb the barren hill to the fort, a rough earthwork, crumbling already to ruins, — only a wall of sods, a ditch, a bastion, — can it be that a fiery tide of life and death so lately seethed around it? Standing on the wall, Knoxville, with her battlements of mountains, her hills, her woods, her waters, and the whole plan of siege, attack, and defence, is revealed. The marks of battle surround us. Large and elegant houses are standing near, from whose grounds every vestige of shrubbery has disappeared. Broad and shapely terraces adorn the hillside, from which the house has been burned to give our guns good range. Opposite on the far horizon we can just discern a house, from which it was discovered that sharpshooters were annoying our men, and the next moment a shell went crashing through its turret and the annoyance ceased. We have heard of the wonderful range of our guns, but here I *see* the distance and do not more than half believe it. The rebel camping-grounds lie before us, hundreds of acres of timber felled for range and breastworks, miles of intrenchments stretching right and left. Every hill has its fort, every valley its rifle-pits, and every wood its regiment, till it seems as if the whole earth was fitted up for a slaughter-house.

Out from yonder woods up this hill came the valiant soldiers, rebels but Americans, brave in a bad cause, — three brigades of picked men, advancing swiftly to storm the fort in the twilight of the dawn. They had planned a surprise, but our men were ready. The fort was manned by eighty-nine men, — another says fifty, — but at any rate the garrison was fearfully small, and the rear of the fort almost undefended. On the outside of the ditch that yawns at our feet as we stand upon the bastion was stretched a small wire about the size of a telegraph wire, and perhaps a foot from the ground. In the darkness it would not be seen, nor at any time would it be likely to be discerned in the fury of attack. The enemy rushed up the hill, till within almost grappling distance, and then our ranks opened upon them a deadly fire. They wavered, they fell, right and left, but still they rushed on, only in the last hot, eager moment to stumble over the treacherous wire headlong into the ditch. Even the gravity of the occasion hardly hides the ridiculousness of the device. It seems like a leaf out of Knickerbocker's History, this Yankee notion of tripping up an army, but it worked fatally well in fact. The men had made up their minds doubtless to leap into the ditch, but pitching in head-foremost they had not counted on. The guns could not of course be trained upon them, but shells were lighted from cigars and flung into the writhing, struggling, raging mass. It is horrible to think of, but as a stratagem its success was complete. The fall, the surprise, the confusion were too much. They would have faced, they did face, known dangers unflinching, but this unexpected and inexplicable shock overset them morally as well as physically. Had they followed the ditch around to the rear of the fort, its capture would have been imminent, but this was not to be. The incessant, fierce fire left them no breathing-space to collect their scattered senses. The strange horror and the frightful carnage together appalled them, and the day was lost.*

But there were deeds of hopeless daring. Some gained the ramparts only to meet certain death. Two men stood before a gun, flung their arms around it, and demanded a surrender. The gun itself replied, and they made no second summons. Once, twice, thrice the Rebel flag was planted on the parapet, and instantly

* A soldier tells the story thus: —

"But little did old Longstreet know
The boys he had to meet him;
They fought on old Virginia's soil,
At Bull Run and Antietam.
The Western boys from Illinois
And Buckeyes won't knock under;
And Yankee steel, it made them squeal,
And Old Kentuck, by thunder!

"The Rebels made a bold advance,
To bag us they intended;
And up the hill on double-quick
The chivalry ascended.

torn away. The hillside was strewn with the dead and dying men. They dropped back from the ramparts. They choked the ditch. The earth was drenched with blood. O God, grant our land may never see such sight again! But Burnside must hold on.

Scarcely a spot around Knoxville that has not its treasured memories, and many generations will listen to the story of her wild warfare. The sufferings, the devotion, and the courage of East Tennessee form no inconsiderable chapter in the history of the great rebellion, — and the armies of the Tennessee, the Cumberland, and the Ohio have left a glorious record on

Our battery's fire, and Burnside's wire,
  It caused them for to stumble,
And head o'er heels into the ditch
  Like 'bullfrogs' they did tumble.

" Our boys did quickly on them pile,
  Amid the great confusion,
Resolved that they should pay the cost
  For such a bold intrusion;
And if, my friends, I have received
  The proper information,
The Rebs will never charge again
  That charged on that occasion."

her rocks. Besides its associations, the town has its own attractions in the rugged natural beauty of the surrounding scenery. Fort Lee affords an exceedingly interesting landscape. It overlooks the intervening ridges, takes in the mountains on both sides, and commands the valley up and down as far as eye can reach. From Fort Haskell we have another magnificent view, — a great sweep of purple mountains, the near green hills, the splendid sunset sky and river, and Knoxville nestling in the valley in the lovely enchantment of distance. But Linden saw another sight, for in this lonely fort, far from houses or roads, accessible only by sheer climbing, crouches a white family, two women and a child, with ashen faces that haunt me yet. This is home. Their clothing is of the scantiest, there is no palpable shelter except the powder-magazine, and they have only the implements of the rudest domestic life. Unless the war helps *them*, what shall recompense us for the war?

Knoxville, like Nashville and Chattanooga, has its soldiers' cemetery, rows upon rows of graves, more than twenty-five hundred, each with its white slab at the head, marked with the name of him who lies under its shadow, or sometimes bearing only the one word "*Unknown.*" Unknown yet well known. In their place are rows of graves, with the little word "*Rebel*" under the name, distinguished by no other mark from the neighboring graves. I am glad to see this, for so it suits a great nation. In war he who lifts his hand against his country is her foe, whether of her own or foreign blood; but when the fighting has ceased they are all her children again, — rebellious children, but her own. Let the bones of the dead be gathered with great sorrow and laid decently in their last resting-place. If there must be reviling and revenge and petty spite, let it not come from the nation which only calmness befits, and composure, and an inexhaustible beneficence.

And so many of these knew not what they did. I think the poverty and the misery of the South — perhaps I ought to say in the South — make a deeper impression on the traveller than anything else. I do not know how much may be the effect of the war, but I fancy a great deal dates farther back than that.

However wasted the land may be by the tramp of armies, it is no four years' war that has spread the dull pallor over the faces I have seen. The wretched cabins bear indubitable marks of time. It is habit, not a sudden absence of occupation, that fills the rickety stoops of rickety taverns with unclean, idle men, and sets in every door-way female figures that have no vestige of female comeliness. I do not think the people of the North have at any time, before, dur ing, or since the war, harbored hatred towards the people of the South; but if ever so bitter or revengeful feelings had been engendered by the strife, there needs but a journey through the South to drive it all away. There can be no resentment, no indignation, nothing but the sorest pity, towards such poverty as we see, such ignorance as we infer. What could these know of loyalty or duty? They *were* loyal to their highest. I only wonder that the South could have drawn its valiant armies from such a rural population as hers. Human nature must be tenacious of its nobility if it can survive such degradation, — if endurance and self-sacrifice and every form of heroism can come out of these Nazareths. We know that nobility does survive, yet there is a fearful waste. We see now how Andersonville was possible.

If there could only be some way devised by which these people could know that there is any other state of society than their own,— could know how differently live the farmers and artisans of the North. Even the excessive toil and care of New England are more hopeful than this idleness and unthrift. We laugh at our staring white cottages, and they are staring, — but the neat little white cottages with their green yards and trim fences are pleasanter to the eye than comfortless cabins. There is no cause for boasting. We are one country, and whatever keeps the South down keeps the North down too. Nothing is injurious to one section that is not before the end, and long before the end, injurious to the other.

My plan of reconstruction would be to gather the poor whites together and send them on an excursion through our New England villages, show them the houses inside and out, the dairies, the larders, the clothes-presses, the tables, the sitting-rooms, the gardens and farms of the common people, and say to them: "This is the very worst we desire for you. All the stories you have heard of our designs of invasion and desecration and subjugation are falsehoods. Through the whole North there is but one wish, — even the wildest Radicals and Fanatics, wise or unwise, wish nothing worse than this, — that you should have every comfort and every freedom that we possess, and that from this starting-point North and South should press forward together."

Some such free intermingling of section with section is necessary to correct the mistakes into which they have fallen. There are so many men — not so very many, perhaps, but what there are make a prodigious din — who design and desire only their own personal aggrandizement, and whose selfishness leads them to believe the lie, that what is worst for others can be made best for themselves, — who therefore find their account in stirring up strife and keeping alive the embers of hatred, — that I see no hope unless the people can be somehow detached from their false guides, and prove for themselves how true and hearty is the good-will which the heart of the North bears the South. Mistaken we may often be in our measures, but if once, in spite of false politicians, the great body of the Southern people could be convinced that the great body of the Northern people wish them only good, it seems to me that wise measures could be speedily agreed upon on both sides.

Here is a Southern paper, which affirms that according to the census one in forty and a half of the entire population of New England are paupers, and one in one hundred and seventy-three criminals; while in the six States of Mississippi, Tennessee, Alabama, Georgia, North Carolina, and Virginia, one in four hundred and fifty-one are paupers, and one in three thousand four hundred and twenty-three criminals. This state of things is held up as a "damaging contrast to our enlightened New England," and the inference drawn is that the six Southern States are by so much in advance of the six Northern States in point of comfort and morality. Now I suppose that no Northern man is deceived by this showing, but I can conceive that a very large part of the South should be. The true significance of the facts will hardly reach the ears that have heard their false application. What we want is, that the truth of facts should somehow be brought to their heads, and the truth of feelings to their hearts; that thus their ambition and aspiration should be touched, and themselves awakened to the possibility of a better life. We need of all things to win the good-will of the South. It is no easy task. An immense crop of hatred has been springing up for years. It was sedulously cultivated during the war, and it must be very long before it will entirely disappear. Our part is to exercise the utmost forbearance. Our strength and courage and determination were abundantly proved by the war; there can be no suspicion of weakness, or cowardice, or lukewarm love of justice, or dignity, in forbearing now. Our papers sometimes quote fierce, wild, hateful, and hating words from Southern journals. I cannot see the good of it. Why not take it for granted that they do hate us bitterly, and then let it alone? While I do not think there is a particle of revenge in the bosom of the North, I think there is a certain impatience and vexation at the persistent hostile and inappeasable attitude of the South. But the indulgence of such sentiments is unworthy both of our education and our religion. The Southern people misunderstand. They know not what they do. If our enlightenment be indeed greater than theirs, we ought to show it in broader and more generous souls. If we are provoked into recrimination, we lower to the level of those who give the provocation.

We were victorious, and on that account also we ought to cultivate an untiring consideration. One feels this through all his soul at Chattanooga. There they live, Southern men and women, — on their own grounds, in their own homes, and everywhere before them the fields of their defeat. They cannot look up but their eyes rest on lost battle-grounds. Every landscape has its story of disaster. The soldiers of the hated conquerors are coming in and going out before them. Visitors are arriving solely to survey the scene of their misfortunes, and departing to spread the tale abroad. We too had our defeats, but they did not come into our door-yards. We do not lie down and rise up with them. And moreover we gained the final victory. They risked all, and lost. Now, I would not compromise one claim demanded by national justice or national safety, but further than this I would not go. If they wish to support Mrs. Davis and her children, let them. If they want to strew the graves of their soldiers with flowers, by all means let them. If they leave the graves of our soldiers unadorned, what matter, since the nation holds them, and the future will hold them in highest honor? If women wish to walk in the middle of the streets, up to their ankles in mud and mire, following the funeral train of a favorite general, why lisp a syllable to oppose them? From the red-heat of war all inflammable substance must be excluded; but now that bloodshed at least is over, I should say the quickest way to put the fire out is to let it burn itself out! These things lay hold of their deepest, truest, tenderest sentiments. The lost cause doubtless to a vast majority was a holy cause. By tact and unswerving courtesy, by a judicious avoidance of topics that arouse useless contention, by quietly attending to those points on which we are agreed, by inducing as far as possible a harmony of interests, by an unobtrusive and untiring expression of good feeling, by a sedulous cultivation of that spirit of Christian love which seeketh not its own, and is not easily provoked, let us endeavor to win them away from their disappointment and unfriendliness, that South and North may be what it never yet has been, one country, one in a higher sentiment than we have ever felt, one in a truer prosperity than we have ever found, one in a nobler destiny than the world has ever seen.

I do not greatly wonder at the feeling compounded of dislike and contempt which the "higher classes" of the South entertain for "Yankees," — apart from their persistent and successful opposition to the peculiar institution. I suspect that very many of the Northerners who go South are ignorant or careless of good breeding, which in its last analysis is Christianity. Christianity in social intercourse demands that you make your neighbor's case your own. Good breeding demands that you act as if you did, whether you do or not. I do not lay this down as a definition for immortality, but it answers my purpose. So then, while a failure in Christianity may go undetected under cover of good breeding, a failure in good breeding is necessarily the failure of Christianity too. I think, therefore, that if one is thoroughly imbued with the spirit of Christianity, while he may fall into awkward mistakes of etiquette disadvantageous to himself, he will never be guilty of those brutal violations of etiquette which awaken resentment in others. But I fear many of our southward travelling citizens are not of the most winning or the most wise character. In the first place, doubtless, many of them do not come from the best people at home, — the people who have attained the last results of Christian refinement and education. They are men of energy, men of honesty, — let us hope, though after the late exhibitions of dishonesty in orthodox circles one can but speak with misgiving, — men of loyalty and anti-slavery, and free-school, and prohibitory liquor-law, and all the rest that we were born to, and have grown up in, and adopted without thought, and fight for in season and out of season; but they are not always men of nice perception, of delicate sensibilities, of quick discrimination as to times, persons, and places. Perhaps they are people who have made their own way in the world, and have become a little roughened by rough usage, as people always are unless provided with safeguards. Or perhaps they are fashioned originally of delft, not porcelain. They take with them the same lack of manners which so disagreeably characterizes the North, — or, if that is too strong, I will say which is so common in the North. Here let me assert, in parenthesis, that from the railroad point of view the South is unquestionably superior to the North. Official persons on the great lines of travel, drivers, conductors, clerks, are usually more attentive. They do their duty more thoroughly. I have heard it suggested that there have been too many men killed for want of decency in small things to render any coarse manners entirely safe. Peaceable folk get the benefit of an improved state of affairs. It may be so, and certainly if the shooting of one in ten of all persons at the North would result in the uniform courtesy of the other nine, one might lay down one's life in a worse cause!

These people go South either to advance their own fortunes or to benefit the South. Sometimes they think to conciliate the Southerners by the expression of a sympathy and pity, which, however innocently intended, is received as insult added to injury. Or they talk loudly of the superiority of Northern to Southern society, — possibly in those very points in which they are themselves deficient. So they awaken antipathy before they have time to command respect. On trial they would prove themselves true friends, and in many respects valuable citizens, but somehow they have not the power to walk softly. Much good they will do, but much also they will fail to do. They will elevate the ignorant, but they will not conciliate the educated. If a missionary should go to the Feejee Islands, I suppose he would hardly say to the Islanders, "Come now, ye pagans, cannibals, savages, and be enlightened by me." The most brutalized heathen is not won by being told that he is a heathen. Think then of the religious devoutness and the elegant manners to be found in the South, — and imagine a "Yankee" as yet somewhat in the rough affirming in its presence that what the South wants is Northern civilization and Northern Christianity! For me, I take issue with the fact, as well as with the mode of expressing it. Neither Northern civilization nor Northern Christianity has ever seemed to me to be of a type so perfect as to justify transportation. I have seen too many and too grievous flaws in both to be very complacent in reflecting on them. Bible Christianity and Bible civilization the South unquestionably wants, and of both she doubtless has a greater lack than the North. If the North can help her to them, so much the better; she will at the same time be helping herself, and, despite her increased possessions, she also stands in sore need of them. But the cause of neither South nor North will be helped by high-sounding proclamations, which have the air, if not the reality, of vainglory.

The South is an excellent specific to put one in humor with the West. An ill-tempered irritable person like — well, let us say like the reader! — does sometimes, it must be confessed, come into contact with the energies of the West almost too violently for his serenity. "You may be the Great West," mentally apostrophizes this violent-tempered person after a doleful day's ride in an unclean and unventilated rail-car, or a day's sail on a Floating Palace, — "you may be the Great West, but you are a very dirty Great West. You are a smoking and a swearing and an uncouth Great West. You are a loose-jointed, ungainly giant, striding over the prairies, leaving your footprints everywhere, brandishing your big arms and bawling out your prowess through the disgusted world. Energy have you? Yes, you are drunken with energy. You are wrecked on the rock of material prosperity. You make it your idol, and you bow down and worship it, sacrificing to it whatever is lovely and fine and thorough. Give over your boasting. I detest material prosperity. Blessed be poverty and failure and calmness and silence. Away with success and population and grain-elevators!

"It is not growing like a tree,
In bulk, doth make man better be,
Or standing long an oak three hundred year,
To fall, a log, at last, brown, bald, and sear.
A lily of a day
Is fairer far in May.
Although it fall and die that night,
It was the plant and flower of light.
In small proportion we just beauties see,
And in short measure life may perfect be."

But hush! infuriated gentle reader. All in good time. We must creep before we walk. And the West is showing such strength of limb and suppleness of joint in creeping, that we may confidently count on her walking both sister and wife of the gods when she does find her feet. Look at poor little Chicago even, — one pities her floundering helplessly in the mud; but is she floundering helplessly? Once, twice, thrice, she has turned to with a will and lifted herself out of the mud unto comparatively clean habitations. She was athirst, and she presently bored a hole two miles long under the lake to get pure water. It is uncomfortable waiting in her dismal railroad station, but just yonder is rising a railroad station that is to be, both in beauty and comfort, monarch of all it surveys, and of much that it cannot survey. This is true civilization, — this bringing the comforts and the elegances of life within everybody's reach. It is because the West is not a land of great performance merely, but of magnificent promise, that we rejoice in it. The time of her madness is gone by, the time when she was called a "Garden of Eden, where the 'land flows with milk and honey,' — where a man has but to 'open wide his mouth, to have it filled with the finest of wheat,'" — when it was declared that "nothing but a parcel of 'old fogies' will be found in Vermont five years hence"; she promises now only what she has power to perform. If the West were con tent with her present attainments, we should be little proud of her, but because these are only stepping-stones to her future greatness we rejoice; because her material prosperity is but the solid basis for a society which shall be the home of all things lovely and of good report, where science and art and religion shall flourish like a green bay-tree, — a society wherein all that is crude shall be mellowed, all that is harsh softened, all that is incomplete rounded into symmetry, till the Great West shall be as graceful as she is prosperous, a centre of light as well as of heat, — the king's daughter, all glorious within.

At the South one sees the need of that very energy which so superabounds in the West. Better that energy should run riot, than that it should die into quiescence and hopelessness. Yet energy there must be in the South, or it never would have carried on its long war so bravely and persistently. What she now wants to develop her great resources is simply opportunity. There needs above all things peace,—a settled condition of things, a knowledge of what is to be depended on. This State of Tennessee abounds in natural wealth. Her valleys are as fertile as they are beautiful. Her woods are inexhaustible. Her marble is already famous. Her quarries would at the North make the fortune of their proprietor. The very stones by the roadside are lumps of copper. East Tennessee is one mass of wealth to him who can make it available. Her unparalleled sufferings, her bravery, her fortitude, and her courage during the war gave her a romantic interest at the North. Peace has not yet brought her quiet. Still, afflicted and impoverished, overrun by the armies of both sides, torn by internal strife, it is easy to see that she has wonderful recuperative powers. Possessing all the elements of beauty, wealth, and health, she must be capable of the highest order of development. Her objectionable features are temporary, her desirable ones lasting.

I cannot but think it a most unfortunate circumstance for the Republican cause in Tennessee, that it has fallen into the hands of the violent, vindictive, and vulgar person at the head of her affairs. Governor Brownlow at the North stands in some sort as representative of the loyalty and patriotism of East Tennessee, — faithful among many faithless. But I believe that no man's good reputation rests on a basis more frail and insecure than his; while the recklessness, profanity, and uncleanness of his speech are such, that it is difficult to conceive of any combination of circumstances which should make it the duty of any man to propose or support him as leader in any measure affecting the welfare of society.

The columns of his own newspaper furnish the authority for my statements, — perhaps I ought rather to say the grounds of my belief.

I think no one who had travelled in the South could ever clamor for her punishment, or feel that she has been let off lightly. Her punishment has long been heavy upon her. She staked all and lost, and now, sitting in dust and ashes, she calls forth no harsher feeling than commiseration. Those men are hardly the truest patriots who talk most loudly of extreme measures for the South, and count all lenity as treachery; but rather they who, yielding nothing to rebellion, strive now only to bind up her bleeding wounds and restore her wasted strength.

CHAPTER X.

East Tennessee. — Historic Doubts concerning Black Mountain. — Footprints of Fugitives. — On the War-trail. — Pursuit of Knowledge under Difficulties. — A Georgian Planter. — Plantation Opinions. — Off the Track. — Northern Man with Southern Experience. — Accounts from Charleston.

UP the East Tennessee valley. The Cumberland Mountains are on our left, and on our right another range, parallel or nearly so with the Cumberland, and averaging about eighty miles apart. This constitutes the eastern wall of the valley and the legal boundary of Tennessee, — mountains of many names, Stone, Iron, Bald, Great Smoky Unaka, Unicay, or Unicai; and somewhere yonder rises the boasted Black Mountain, which is said to have wrested the championship from our Mount Washington, but I am not yet convinced. It is a beautiful valley that we are traversing, watered by the Holston, the Clinch, the Nolichuckey, and numerous other rivers, all bringing their largess of loveliness and wealth. In this region they point out the tree on which was hung the first victim of the rebellion in Tennessee; and Greenville, late home of the President; and the roof of the house in which the guerilla Morgan was shot. Here too you see what none show, — the hosts of war-worn fugitives fleeing from rebel prisons, coming

> "Through the jaws of death,
> Back from the mouth of Hell,"

seeking the shelter of the old Flag. O the aching feet that have climbed these mountain-sides, the fearful eyes that have seen a pursuer in every shadow, the brave hearts that have held on through every danger! It seems almost pusillanimous to have sat quietly at home all through the thunder-storm of battle, and, as soon as the cloud had discharged its death-bolts, to come riding as quietly over the fields of its devastation, just to look at them.

On and on, up and down, we are in the famous valley of Virginia, past Mount Airy, past the "Peaks of Otter," lifting their heads high above the surrounding scenery, with the gap between marking the line of retreat pursued by General Hunter when foiled in his effort to capture Lynchburg. Some we see by day and some by night, ghostly and grand in the bright moonlight, — for there is but one train a day on the railroad, and travellers have no choice of light or darkness. But the sleeping-car is luxuriously easy, and gives rest if not sleep.

There is pleasant talk, too, in the long journey. I hear no words of bitterness or hatred, scarcely any politics or any allusion to the war. Only an elderly gentleman scowls upon the boy who offers him a Harper's Monthly for sale, and affirms rather ostentatiously that he does not allow it in his house! And a young man and his wife, of middling position, have a contemptuous word to say to each other about the "Yankees," which they could be taught to unsay in ten minutes. There is a pretty girl opposite, travelling with her newly-married husband, the purple and fine linen of her bridal outfit as yet all unassoiled. Down the car is a family group migrating eastward, two grown girls among them, chattering their musical nothings with the inexhaustible light-heartedness of youth and good spirits.

On a seat next a window sits a young woman alone, and in front of her a man alone. He was evidently originally intended to be handsome after a large and generous sort, but a coarse, not to say a dissipated life, has robbed him of every vestige of beauty. Moreover he is not neatly dressed, and altogether is not pleasing. The woman I have never seen before, but the man has been travelling some distance our way, and soon after his appearance was pointed out as a person of distinction, elected to high office by a Southern State, and of some national prominence. Of course I am interested in him. I am near, and I can see him without looking, and in any lull of the train I cannot help hearing all that is said. What I do hear furnishes a charming offset to Yankee inquisitiveness. The man has several newspapers lying on the seat and over its back. In one of our many pauses the young woman asks permission to look at a paper. He grants it graciously, but in a gruff and peculiarly hollow voice, that reminds one of his youthful experiments of talking into an empty barrel. Presently she returns the paper with thanks. After a while he offers her another, which she declines with thanks. Then I smile inwardly, to see him half glancing at her from under his shaggy eyebrows, and now and then turning half around to her, evidently making up his mind to speak. It is always so easy to see what a man wants to do when you stand aloof yourself. She gazes all the while tranquilly out of window, but I make no doubt is quite as aware as I am of everything going on. Presently he can contain himself no longer, and opens the ball.

"Travelling South?"

"No sir," with the slightest possible start of surprise that does not in the least deceive me. "I am going to Washington."

"Do you live in Washington?"

"No sir,"—a half-pause, but evidently not wishing palpably to snub him. "I live in New Hampshire."

"What part of New Hampshire?"

"The southwestern part, near Keene." (A "Yankee school-ma'am," I say to myself.)

"Name of town?"

Half annoyed and half amused, she perhaps gives the name of the town, but I do not catch it, neither I think does he, yet he has not the smallest suspicion of being repulsed. If he thinks anything, he doubtless thinks she is shy, and needs to be drawn out by an affable interlocutor like himself. Her face I cannot wholly see, but I imagine her "mingled emotions" as his character gradually reveals itself. As a companion he is not agreeable, but as a phenomenon he is worth observing.

"Visiting in the South?"

"Yes sir, and in the West. I have been in Cincinnati and around through Nashville, Chattanooga, and Knoxville." (This detour is necessary to all travellers this way, there being but one railroad as yet, though I believe one is projected directly through from Cincinnati to Knoxville, and so to Washington.)

"Ah! relic-hunting!"

"No, not exactly. Rather sight-seeing."

"Any friends in Chattanooga?"

"Yes sir, a few, not many."

He had "made up his mouth" to ask their names, but she turns him aside with some remark that I do not hear, and the next question that comes to my ears is, —

"Travelling alone?"

"No sir, my cousin is with me."

"Travelling with cousin, eh?"

"Yes sir."

He must have found his pursuit of knowledge rather fatiguing, for he forbears further investigation and subsides into semi-somnolence.

In an hour or two we pass a cemetery on a pleasant hillside, and several of the passengers leave their seats to look at it. The young woman in question goes to the rear of the car for a better view, and on her return her obliging neighbor remarks, "Cemetery for the Federal soldiers."

Perhaps she is a little lackadaisical, for she answers, "After life's fitful fever they sleep well."

He gazes at her a moment, evidently struck with the new idea that they all died of fever, and then puts the entirely irrelevant query, —

"Husband ain't along?"

"No sir."

"Left him in Massachusetts?"

"He is there if he is anywhere, doubtless," with a smile only half suppressed.

"Ah! not married, did you say?"

"O no! I did not say that. However, I am not married."

"Young ladies coming from the North generally get caught up pretty quick at the South."

"Then it stands them in hand to stay at home."—But repenting herself of the inference, she adds, "if they don't want to be caught up."

"Did you ever see a young lady that did not want to get married?"

"I don't know that I ever did."

"That 's honest. Never saw one that did not want to get married?"

"No, I did not say that. I don't know that I ever saw one. I do not know what young ladies want."

But I do not reckon this man one of the pearls and corals of deep-sea soundings in the South. He is but a weed temporarily tossed up by the storm.

Our own party is increased and enlivened by the advent of a Georgian planter, a man of the world, shrewd, wealthy, and witty. Yankee shrewdness is proverbial, but when a Southerner gives his mind to it he is a fair match for the

Yankee. Our Georgian friend looks, too, like the ideal Yankee. He is tall, and slender, and sallow, — enfeebled just now by a recent illness. He seems to be conversant with the whole country. He is interested in developing mines in Georgia. He has dealings in Tennessee also, and both the Carolinas, — and he expresses himself with great freedom. "It was a most needless war," he says, — "a wanton war. It never ought to have been fought. It was brought on by unprincipled men, — your side as well as mine," with a playful, defiant nod at us Yankees. "It was not a people's war. It was a politician's war. Look at —— State. Take all the papers that were blatant for secession. How many of them represented any material interest? Not one. They were managed by a set of poor devils who had nothing to lose. The rich men knew that the war meant ruin, and they went dead against it, but they were powerless. What is the result? Just what was prophesied. They sold themselves, and lost the niggers."

In one sense, doubtless, the war was a needless war, but in another sense it was inevitable.

The alleged provocations were insufficient to induce an appeal to arms, but in the great march of events — human nature being what it is, and human development at its present stage — we had come to a point where no further progress could be made without collision. The causes of the war lay far below its occasion, far below the power of politicians materially to hurry or hinder. Perhaps we shall understand this better a thousand years hence than now.

"Look at what the war has done for us," adds the ireful Georgian. "Here is East Tennessee that you have just seen, — a heaven-favored valley, but where is it now? Bad men who cared only for their own pockets took the lead in the rebellion, protested long and loud their loyalty to the South, and so got the ear of the Confederate authorities and dictated the policy for this, to them, disloyal population. They perpetrated revolting outrages upon the unprotected Union men, and when their reign was over the Unionists suffered again at the hands of their friends. Men who had been honest citizens before the war came back from the Federal army, to which they had fled for protection, demoralized by camp life and determined to revenge themselves on those who had forced them away from their homes, and they went for those who should grant the greatest latitude to their vengeance. Being allowed to prey first upon their enemies' property, as a punishment for real or imaginary wrongs, the whole thing soon sunk into a general system of plunder, carried on by gross violence. Men have been killed, mobbed, exiled, from no higher motive than pelf. Indeed, for a time violence and dishonesty got the upper hand entirely, and the tendency was to the wildest excesses. Men who did not like to steal outright did it under color of law. Courts were organized, narrow-minded, illiterate, incompetent men were placed on the bench, and such another crop of litigation as sprang up there you must go far to find."

"But this state of things is giving way to something better?"

"Things are bad enough now. The internal affairs of the State are in a most unsettled condition. It affects the simplest matters of business. Nobody knows what to look for, and therefore nobody knows what to do."

"What is the remedy, in your judgment?"

"The true policy was that foreshadowed by President Lincoln, and the terms of capitulation conceded by Grant. Had this been acted upon in its broadest sense and guaranteed by universal amnesty, we should to-day, in my opinion, have been the most united, harmonious, and prosperous people on earth. The South was conquered, and in a temper to have appreciated and responded to a generous forbearance on the part of the North with a warmth of gratitude and national pride that would have electrified the nation. Their defeat, losses, and sufferings had already begun to engender a feeling of hatred against the men who had betrayed them into rebellion. A little encouragement would have kindled this lurking dissatisfaction into open denunciation, and peace would have come at once. But distrust aggravated by falsehood, short-sightedness, and party machinations intervened and forbade the banns, and here we are drawing wider and wider apart."

"But what do you consider the exciting cause of this distrust? What was it that prevented the —"

"I will tell you what it was. Politicians — men who prize place more than they do the public good — fancied that the restoration of the Southern States would displace them from power. Under this conviction, and with the view of retaining power and controlling and carrying the next Presidential election, they deliberately set themselves to work to prevent a restoration."

I asked him of the President. President and Congress he believed to be acting from one and the same motive, self-aggrandizement, and as their objects are world-wide apart there could but be a quarrel. "All the advantage the President has over Congress is that he is nearer right than they. The quarrel itself must display the workings of the spirit that produced it, a disregard of truth and the decencies of official position and intercourse, intolerance, vituperation, and a wanton trampling under foot of official oaths. Everything seems to be done with an eye single to the advancement of party till the Constitution is already, so far as Congress is concerned, abrogated, and there is no limit to Congressional action except the capricious Congressional will, which is animated and controlled by petty malice and narrow views of party policy. What we want is a statesman who can rise far enough above personal considerations to point out the road to safety. I do not care for his residence or his former party predilections, if he is only capable, true, and patriotic."

I asked him what attitude he took at the commencement of the struggle.

"For twenty years," he answered, "I warred against the growing spirit of alienation, the tendency to national disruption, — but to no purpose. When the conflict began, I deplored it more than any act of madness our countrymen had ever perpetrated, and I did all I could to avert it. But of course I could not hate the Southern people. The influence of many others throughout the South was exerted in favor of the maintenance of the authority of the Federal Government. We believed the solemn declaration of Congress that the war was waged for the preservation of the government and the Union, and we did not believe that men like myself had forfeited any of our constitutional rights; we believed, if treason was a crime, it was the crime of those who committed it, and not the crime of the State, and that, as the Federal army approached, it would be an army of liberation, and not of oppression; that it would bring with it the protection which the Constitution guarantees to every American citizen, to every loyal man residing in the South. We were willing to bear all the inevitable evils incident to war, and to submit to such changes in the fundamental law as were necessary to secure the future safety of the country. So we not only acquiesced, but aided, in the abolition of slavery. Beyond this we were unwilling to go."

"How were your own slaves affected by the war?"

"I said to them in the beginning: 'You are going to be free. The war is going to free you all. You stay at home and behave yourselves. Don't you go to cutting up, and don't you go into the army.' Not one of them left me. They knew I was their friend. I never flogged my slaves. If they stole, I sold them, that 's all, and no words about it. When the time came,

I bought farms and put some of my men on, and set them up for themselves. I got places for some of them, and some I hire. They come to me now when they want anything. About all owe me money, five or ten dollars apiece. I think it is better to lend them money than give it to them, because they don't come so often. They are afraid, if they ask for more, I shall ask them to pay what they borrowed before. I had no trouble with my slaves through the war. They would do anything for me, — ride fifty miles by night alone if I asked them. I had one of them to help me bury my silver at night. He and I went out together. He was the only one that knew anything where it was. When peace came, he went with me and got it out again."

I asked how he bore himself towards the war.

"I kept everybody out of it that I could. I advised every one over whom I had any influence not to go into the army. Whenever I found any fugitive, Union prisoner, or rebel soldier lurking about my grounds, I fed him. My servants had orders to feed everybody that wanted food."

Was he always furnished with food?

"Always. I looked out for that in the first place. I had hams laid up for a regiment. I laid up store for two years ahead. I could have held out a good while longer than the war did. I advised against taking the Confederate Bonds. I knew they were worthless. To be sure nobody believed me, and went on just the same. They said, if we succeeded, the Confederate Bonds would be as good as cotton or gold. If we failed, all the land would be confiscated, and therefore real estate would be worth no more than bonds. There was a possibility of gain on one side, and a certainty of loss on the other. I took Confederate Bonds to pay my debts and buy plantations with. That is all the use I ever had for them."

"But are your plantations good property now?"

"Not now. They are doing very little yet; but they are as good as anything, and will be better if the country is ever settled. But nothing can be done so long as we are in this distracted and uncertain condition."

The train has been standing still in the woods a long while, from some unexplained cause. But we do not object; it is a pleasant place, and the cessation of the whiz and whir is a relief to the ear. In the pauses of our talk I hear the ripple of an unseen brook by the roadside. It turns out that we have run over, or rather have tossed up a cow, and she in return has tossed the tender off the track. Many cows have had hair-breadth escapes from us to relate to their listening calves on some future summer eve, but this is the first one who has proved in her own experience the truth of George Stephenson's answer to the incredulous and somewhat sneering Parliamentary Committee, who asked him if it would not be a very awkward circumstance should a cow stray upon the track and get in the way of the engine. "Very awkward indeed—*for the coo!*"

"Plantations," says another planter, joining in the conversation, — a Northern young man who went from college to the war, and after the war remained — one can hardly say "settled" — in South Carolina, leasing plantations and tilling them with his own brains and money, — "plantations are of very little use without money. I know of people in South Carolina who were millionnaires before the war, and who have plantations by the dozen now, but are utterly cleaned out of ready money."

"Yes," said the Georgian, "a few persons have preserved their property, but very few."

"It must make a vast difference in the whole state of society?"

"I should think so," said the Northern planter. "I do not know how it used to be, — the aborigines hold themselves much aloof from the invaders, — but going to Charleston from the North is like going back a hundred years. The forced economy, simplicity, and quiet are very striking. Houses all old, but most of them large, commodious, and picturesque. No street lights, worse than no street pavements, no private carriages, no theatres or other public amusements (not even a sensation preacher). People wear any sort of clothes, old Confederate uniforms, sometimes with the buttons altered, sometimes not, 'jeans,' and other homespuns. Kid gloves are almost unknown. Girls go to parties at eight, wearing high-necked muslin dresses, and sup on cake and sangaree. The conductors of the street cars are young gentlemen, — real ones.

Family equipages, if there ever were any, have disappeared."

"Not six," added the Georgian emphatically, "in this town, that formerly boasted two hundred."

"Do they submit to this state of things, or do they struggle against it?"

"They take to it rather kindly than otherwise. There is very general stagnation. People have nothing to do, and give themselves plenty of time to do it. The burnt district still lies empty. In the ruined tower of a church near my town boarding-house I have heard the screech-owl. The people are prostrate and despairing. They confess themselves a conquered country and ready to suffer anything. They seem to live in the memories of the past, consoling themselves with having made a good fight in a bad cause, and boasting like Palmerin of England in the giant's castle: 'Certes, it can never be said of me, that, using my strength, I was conquered to my shame!'"

"One cause is," said the Georgian, "that the people are utter disbelievers in republican government, and convinced that the United States *must* go to the deuce some day, however prosperous at present."

"I think, however," said the Northerner, "that the men are rather more inclined to reconstruction than the women."

Of course I put in a word of explanation here, which it is not necessary to report. What I desire is simply to present the unstudied opinions of honest men who are neither partisans nor politicians, — the opinions that are given in common conversation, which seem to me far more valuable than public set speeches.

"I know," continued the younger planter, "some desperate fire-eaters, renowned duellists, whom I now regard as Christian did Giants Pope and Pagan. The war has cut the claws of many such giants. Do you remember how, in the old dramatists (Marlowe's Edward II. is a good example), the character who is revelling in wicked power at the beginning is so ill-treated before the end, that you forget his old offences and he attracts all your sympathy? That is the way these Charlestonians affect me now; and I do not like the idea of their being exterminated piecemeal, as a cat kills a mouse, by the triumphant, power-intoxicated Congressional majority."

"Half the talk about the negro," said the Georgian, "is mere humbug, to keep up that abominable system of robbery called 'protection.'"

"Abominable indeed," I echo, sympathetically.

"What do *you* know about it?" he queries, glowering at me, good-humoredly.

"Everything there is to know," — sacrificing truth to bravado.

We are coming back once more to villages, — Charlottesville with its University, the child of Jefferson's old age, past Monticello, his home, and then through a succession of battle-grounds, scarred still with strife, wrapped now in a deathly quiet. Manassas, Bull Run, — what intensity of life lies hidden in those words, what past and future meet in voiceful silence here!

CHAPTER XI.

In Washington. — Arlington. — Freedmen's Village. — A Patriarch. — Comparing Notes with Freedmen concerning Freedom. — Mount Vernon Colored Schools. — Colored Churches. — A (colored) Representative of the First Families of Virginia. — Gettysburg. — Gossip of the Battle. — Home. — The Dénouement.

YARROW Revisited is never, I suppose, quite the same as Yarrow Visited. Washington has not passed unchanged through the fierce disorders of our battle-years. Peaceful and prosperous enough, her streets have not yet lost the echoes of war, and still on her highlands we see

> "Grandest of mortal sights,
> The sun-browned ranks to view, —
> The Colors ragg'd in a hundred fights,
> And the dusty Frocks of Blue!"

A living presence, he walks here still, the patient, sad-eyed man who led the people through the sea and through the wilderness and was not, for God took him. A spirit broods over these familiar landscapes, and sheds for all time an influence stronger than the gay laugh or the merry word can dispel. There comes over me a great longing to see the old places, — alas! the old faces I shall never see again. Arlington still fronts us from her wooded nest, — Arlington with her pillared stateliness afar, with her cheap finery at hand. The old oaks that have not been despoiled are as beautiful as ever; there are still the noble groves, the broad estate, but it is sown with a more precious seed than ever its owner scattered. All along the drive-way, by the roadside, in grove and garden and field they lie, "comrades of camp and mess," foes in battle, but friends in death, — "Union," "Rebel," "Unknown," tenderly cared for, smiled on by sun, sheltered by shade, sung to by bird and breeze. O,

> "Well may Nature keep
> Equal faith with all who sleep,"

and well may our country emulate Nature enfolding all the dead in her motherly embrace. But a mightier arm than government's holds ownership here, and no reversion of decree can dispossess the speechless hosts that haunt these woods,

> "Unseen, both when we wake and when we sleep."

It is eminently fitting that a part of this estate should be tenanted by the Freedmen. Their little whitewashed village is the picture of neatness. Children are playing in the hard, gravelled streets, and old men are sunning themselves on benches before the door. It is a hazardous thing, this government tutelage, but I suppose it was the only thing to be done, and so it come to an end at the earliest possible moment, I trust it will bring only good. Driving through the village we make occasion to stop and push inquiries, and are soon surrounded by a dozen negroes, chiefly women and children, little black-eyed imps that look irresistibly roguish, but keep a respectful though grinning silence while their elders are talking. We are presently joined by an infirm and very aged man, and "How are you getting on, uncle?"

"Poorly, poorly," with a smile, and a soft, tremulous, low voice.

"Were you also freed by the war?"

"No Mass'r, I was fuss slave in Maryland, den I was sole down in South Carlina. Mass'r, he kep me thar till I was too ole to work, den he freed me, an' gib me money to pay my fare, an' started me Norf again to get to my chil'en."

"Which do you like best, being a freedman or a slave?"

"O, I'd be better with my ole Mass'r. Nobody can take as good care of me as my ole Mass'r. Don't give me money enough now to buy a chaw of tobacky."

This objection to freedom is speedily removed, and the old man is voluble in his gratitude, "God bless you, Sir, and send you to Heaven, Sir." Hurry slowly there, old friend, but tell us does not government help you live?

"O yes! gub'ment gives rations of meat once in five days."

"And how much is a ration?"

"Well, two, free pounds," which seems a very respectable ration after all.

"Can you tell us how old you are, uncle?"

"If I live till this time next year, I shall be a hundred."

Old as he looks, we are a little incredulous of this statement, but he refers us to Mrs. —— in Washington, who knows his age, and will corroborate his assertion.

On our way home our colored driver — colored legally, but his olive complexion, his straight glossy black hair, his dark gray-blue eyes, give no sign of any but the pure blue blood, — is questioned about this matter of freedom. "Are the blacks in Washington really any better off than before they were free?"

He thinks they have more priv'leges.

"Are they intelligent enough to comprehend or appreciate freedom?"

"The blacks is just like other folks; some is perfectly ign'ant, some is apt to learn, and some is intelligent."

"Are they industrious, and do they have a fair chance for a living?"

"Them what's mind to work can do well, an' them what's lazy and hang roun' don' do nothin'."

He distinguishes also between the contrabands and the refugees, the former class comprising those who were freed by the army, and the latter those who came over of their own will from Maryland. One of these he puts quite above the other, but I have forgotten which it is!

Another colored man, formerly a slave on the Mount Vernon estate, when asked his opinion of freedom as compared with slavery, replied demurely, "I ain't no fault to find with my last master."

"That was Mr. Washington."

"No, myself!"

Mount Vernon has been greatly improved since it came into the hands of our countrywomen. On the brightest of all bright autumn days, we visited it, passing through a waste yet lovely country, through the smutty little town of Alexandria, past the slave-pen, past the house where Ellsworth rushed to his death long ago, tarrying to enter the little ivied church where Washington came to worship, and which keeps still in its ancient form the square pew which he occupied. We linger in the shaded church-yard among the quaint inscriptions, and drop a natural tear to the memory of "dorothy harper, who departed this life after and in Dispocion of three years," rejoice with the surviving relatives of another lady in the comfortable reflection that she was connected with several of the most respectable families of Virginia, and mentally chide those mischievous soldier boys, who have made some of these stones tell a different story from what they were set to speak. Then again across the scarcely inhabited country, till we enter the Mount Vernon estate, and drive mile after mile through its magnificent grounds, over broken, rugged, perhaps dangerous, but romantic roads to the beautiful home that Washington loved so well, — the charming, rural home, set in the glory of gay greenwood and sunny slope and velvet sward and winding way, fronting the river and the dam, and wooing to itself all the enchantments of earth and sea and sky. I am glad to see that neatness and order have taken the place of its late unthrift, and restored to it something of the comeliness of its first estate. The turf is smoothed and the walks clean. The old disgraceful untidiness of the tomb is banished, and all things are done decently. Yet I must confess I do not see the necessity of having so large a part of the house closed to visitors. I supposed it was the property of the women of the country, held for the country's honor and benefit; yet of the eighteen rooms that the house contains, we are allowed to see but four or five, — no more than were open when it was in the possession of Mr. Washington. Our conductor informs us that these are the only rooms of any interest, but I would much prefer to judge for myself what rooms have interest. I think Washington's library has a very deep and peculiar interest, but it is used as a dining-room by its present occupant, and is inaccessible. The guest-chambers of Washington cannot be entirely commonplace, but none of them are open to inspection. Indeed, the house seems just as much a private house as when it was in private hands. It may be necessary for safe keeping that a part of the house should be occupied, but certainly its safety might be insured without devoting thirteen or fourteen rooms to its custodians, and leaving only four or five to the world.

For the one colored school that used to be in Washington, a stone of stumbling, and a rock of offence, there are colored schools springing up in various directions, unconcerned and unnoticed. I found them in no respect essentially different from any common country district school. Some of the pupils were bright, and some were dull. Some answered promptly, some hesitatingly, and some not at all. It is as our driver says, "the blacks is just like other folks," and the sooner we become convinced of the fact, and cease special measures and ways of thinking, the better. In the churches, however, there seemed a greater difference between African and American modes than in the schools. One church which we attended was celebrating the Lord's Supper. It was a large house, but the lower part was already filled to overflowing. We went up a narrow, steep flight of stairs, to the galleries. The sexton met us at the head of the stairs, and put to each one who came up the question, "Are you a member?" The "ayes" were conducted to a seat, or at least to a standing-place. The "noes" were very courteously informed, that, owing to the great numbers present, the church was able to provide seats only for "members." The sexton permitted us to remain standing as long as we chose, and seemed particularly to regret his inability to accommodate us. He came to us once or twice, expressed his sorrow, hoped we should not fail to come to them again, and expressly invited those who went away to return in the evening, when there would be room for all. His regrets and apologies were expressed not with servility, but with a gentle, soft-spoken courtesy that was very winning. The services were conducted in an orderly and serious manner. The prayer was fervent, and seemed to spring from a heart conscious of the exigencies of the time. The speaker besought the Lord to "nerve us for the work laid upon us, — that we may not fear frowns nor court smiles." The singing was melodious and energetic. A good many of the congregation kept time with their feet, and the rhythmic thumps seemed to give a sort of emphasis to the ascriptions of praise. As the services went on, we became aware of a certain ground-swell of enthusiasm without any especial exciting cause. There was a swaying and a rocking of the body, an eagerness and a loudness of response, but no ungainly. tumult.

As the numbers increased to a crowd around

us, and as ventilation has not, I regret to say, been carried to any greater perfection in colored churches than in our own, we generously relinquished our standing-places to later comers and went to another church. This was about half full. Several ministers were in the pulpit, tall, stalwart, well-dressed, and good-looking men. The pastor of the church read the notices, but the preacher for that day was a stranger. We missed the first part of the sermon, but the theme seemed to be the deliverance of the Israelites out of Egypt. As might be supposed, the subject would naturally lead to exciting topics, and the congregation showed themselves fully alive to the existing state of things. Their Amens and Glory to God's grew gradually louder and louder, till they became fused into one homogeneous and prolonged "hi! yi!" — a kind of sacred yell recurring at minute intervals during the most exciting passages, and fairly drowning the speaker's words. He fully shared in the excitement which he had kindled. Repeatedly he jumped from the floor as high as he could leap, two or three times in succession, — a gesture more impressive than solemn. His voice, as well as his body, was raised to the highest pitch. "When the Lord wanted to let the Egyptians go, he brought in the elements. When this country was so clogged with slavery that the truth of God was become a lie," — hi! yi! hi! and clerical gymnastics, — "distinguished divines — " Hi! yi! "God removed slavery at once!" Renewed and prolonged yells, during which the preacher's lips seemed to be framing words, and his straining muscles indicated extreme exertion; but there was no distinguishable voice in the storm of sound. The whole congregation seemed to be swaying towards him, drawn unconsciously but irresistibly by a kind of magnetic attraction. One of the occupants of the pulpit, a middle-aged, light-complexioned, gray-whiskered man, who in repose looked as if he might be Secretary of the American Board, or some other equally grave and reverend seignior, seemed to be in an ecstasy. He rubbed his hands, slapped his knees, bobbed his head down almost low enough to meet them, hitched and twisted himself to right and left, jerked his head sidewise, laughed and shouted and talked to himself.

"Eight years ago," said the preacher in ear-splitting tones, "I was stationed here. What a difference between then and now! Now we can come to meeting and go anywhere. Then if I stayed out late I was in danger of being taken up. If I was out to evening meeting after ten o'clock, I was put in the old prison and taken before Squire Deeley, Monday morning, and had to pay *five dollars* and FORTY-NINE CENTS before I could go home!" (Renewed applause.) "Then they talked about our meetings because we made such a growling and racket, but now"—(drowning shouts)—"political smiles and bows, and it's all right." Then he gradually drew away from politics and returned to religion proper, assuring his hearers with great force, and not without eloquence, that "there is no other name given under heaven among men whereby we can be saved, not Europe, nor Asia, nor Ameriky, nor the star-spangled banner, nor any other banner, but the blood-stained banner of the cross!" The discourse was rambling and disconnected, but no more so than the address of any illiterate and unthinking man might have been.

I went afterwards to another church at the

evening service. The first part was a religious, and the second a business meeting. The various officers of the church handed in their reports, which seemed to be minute and satisfactory. The treasurer reported five hundred and fifty dollars in the hands of the trustees, and three hundred and fifty in those of the steward, as the fund for church support, which is certainly a very fair showing, and compares favorably with white churches. A contribution of about twenty dollars was called for. The box is not passed around, but laid on the table, and the people go up and deposit their gifts as the spirit moves them, and different hymns are sung till the work is over. The contributing at this time went on very briskly at first, the preacher reporting the increasing amount from time to time. As it began to slacken he interspersed explanatory and exhortatory remarks. "Sixteen dollars. It may not be perfectly understood what is the object of this contribution, and I will therefore say it is to make out the last quarter of your unworthy servant's salary. Seventeen dollars and a half. I would say to all of you that have not paid, that it is desirable you pay quick.

We don't want it dragging along. We don't want to say anything more about it than is necessary. It is nineteen dollars, and I think we had better stop. We don't want to sing for a dollar." But the people kept on coming till they had contributed a dollar or two beyond the required sum, and were cautioned not to be too generous; so the meeting dissolved in great good humor. But it was by no means an exhibition of the inability of the African race to take care of itself.

Another illustration of its sagacity, was the story that came to me from a colored servant. He was a fine-looking young man, with straight hair and blue eyes. At the North he would never be suspected of any but the true azure blood. His father was of the best Virginia stock. His mother was a slave, and served as cook in a restaurant in a Southern city. When Jack was a year old, a party of drunken revellers at the restaurant were attracted by his cries as he lay in the cradle, and in a fit of maudlin generosity they contributed fifty dollars, bought him, and presented him to his mother.

Being colored, he could not attend school in

his native city; so when he reached his boyhood, he went to Washington, where he submitted his mind to six months' friction, under adverse circumstances, and became a scholar. His mother meanwhile contracted with her owner for her freedom for a stipulated sum. After paying a portion of that from her small savings during several years of hard labor as a slave, she bethought herself of taking advantage of that clause in the Constitution or something else which provides that any slave remaining in the District of Columbia for a year, without returning to Old Virginia, becomes thereby free. Accordingly she established herself in Washington, and by a judicious system of scouting, and the advice and assistance of skilful friends, she managed to elude the affectionate searches of her owner through the specified year, and became at last owner of herself without ever paying the remainder of the debt. Such is the unsettled state of the country at present, and the unreconstructed condition of the negro, that it is to be feared she never will pay it.

Jack next apprenticed himself to a barber, with whom he remained until twenty-one. After the war broke out, he took the stump in meetings of the blacks for recruiting soldiers for the Union army. He did this with the expectation and the promise of a Lieutenancy; but after the troops were raised, the commanding officers of the regiment discovered that he was a descendant of Canaan, and he was denied his office. During the war his influence, his conversation, and his conduct were for the Union.

All this while his deaf and dumb sister was the property of a lawyer in a Virginia village, who retired with his family to Richmond when our army took possession of the village and the lines of the Rebels were contracted. With the return of peace this man returned to his country home. From that place Jack first heard of his sister, although he had vainly tried to learn her whereabouts in Richmond. He was told that she was inhumanly treated by her owner, and he immediately obtained a written permission from the proper officer of the Freedman's Bureau that his sister should accompany him, if she chose, to Washington, and an order from that officer to the commandant of the post at the village, for the necessary military assistance if obstacles were interposed; the next morning after he received his information, he went to find her. When she saw him, such was her joy that she fell fainting into his arms.

Her former owner refused to allow her to return with him. The commandant of the post gave him a sergeant and six men to bring her before him, and allow the claimant to show cause why she should not accompany her brother to Washington. The case was heard in the town hall, and Jack conducted it himself.

The owner admitted that the effect of the Emancipation Proclamation was the destruction of his ownership, but claimed a contract with her for a year's service, which had just begun.

Jack questioned the jurisdiction of the commandant to hear and determine the question of contract, calling the attention of the officer to the fact that the order upon him from his superior was to remove obstacles to the visit to Washington of his, Jack's, sister, if she chose to go; that the question of contract, so far as that tribunal was concerned, was not at issue.

The owner then argued that the girl was born

in his family, and ought to be strongly attached to it; that his children had grown up with her and were attached to her; that she had been kindly cared for, and ought not to think of leaving them for Washington; that Jack was young and could not support her.

Jack replied, that it was not a question of whether he could support her or not, or how she ought to feel, but only how she *did* feel, what she did want to do. Did she want to go to Washington? If she did, obstacles were to be removed.

The owner pleaded that Washington was a bad place, that the girl while in his family had always preserved her character unsullied.

Jack was indignant, and retorted that his sister was as safe with him, her kindred, as with others, and that it was strange if the daughter of his mother could not keep herself unspotted; that the simple inquiry should be whether she wanted to go to Washington or not; that it was a question to be submitted to her, as she alone could decide it. He proposed that she should be placed by herself, apart from the crowd which filled the room, that her claimant might address his deaf and dumb alphabet to her as long as he chose, and he would abide the result.

The Court believed this was right, and ordered the trial. The claimant twisted his fingers in all ways conceivable for half an hour. Jack twisted his half a minute, and she rushed across the room and clung about his neck. The case was concluded, the audience applauded. To the best of my knowledge and belief, there was some crying in the room. At any rate the Court issued the order, and the claimant retired a sadder and a wiser man.

Jack and sister came in triumph to Washington, and the night of their coming was emphasized with thanksgiving and praise by the household and its neighbors.

From Washington to Gettysburg, the little village that sprang suddenly out of obscurity into the forefront of renown. The brilliant sunshine that has attended us everywhere does not fail us here, and the village lies in such unbroken quiet as beseems a true Dutch borough. How utterly incredible that the storm of war should have roared through this placid valley! How utterly incongruous the boom of cannon and the rattle of musketry with the gentle sounds of village industry and burgher thrift! Yet hither the war came, surged up to this peaceful inland town, lifted it from all its commonplace surroundings, and gave it forevermore one of the great historic names. Here rebellion reached high-water mark, and receded into its bottomless pit. But the refluent wave left wreck and refuse which have not yet passed away. The country roads in all directions are strewed with canteens, haversacks, cartridge-boxes, torn shoes, fragments of clothing. The hills are sown with bullets, which every rain reveals. A day or two before our visit, a little girl brought to one of the shops six pounds of bullets, which she had picked up on a hillside after a heavy rain. There are a few houses whose walls, doors, and shutters are well riddled with bullets, but such signs of conflict are far more rare than one would suppose possible after a three days' fight. But Gettysburg was not the object of the struggle, and, securely nestled between her hills, with five miles of battle radiating from her, the bullets whizzed and whistled over her head, and left her for the most part unharmed. It is significant of the difference between North and South, that, while the latter lies desolate as the war left it, this little neighborhood has speedily recovered from its wounds. Fences are rebuilt, fields cultivated, and plenty smiles where so lately war ravaged. The slope of Seminary Ridge is green and pleasant, as if foot of Rebel had never come over it. But down this road they came, having passed around the town to enter it from the north, while our army held the southern approaches. On this road they show the stone cottage which General Lee occupied for his head-quarters. Not far away General Longstreet, I think, established himself, and the terrified women remained in their house during the whole of the first day's fight. At night they begged for an ambulance to take them back into the country beyond the line of battle. The General assured them that his army had advanced so far that they were already out of the line of battle, and there was no need of their leaving home.

"But if you should retreat, General?"

"Ah! Madam, we don't intend to retreat!"

Here is the cupola of some public building, from which General Lee vainly tried to overlook the whole field of what was to be his defeat. The hills beyond the town were higher than any eminence he could command, and those hills, in spite of his brave and desperate charges, remained in the possession of the Union army. Slowly we drive along the public roads, across fields, into lanes, quiet by-ways that seem made for the tinkling of cow-bells and the bleating of lambs, and that must have been surprised at strange, heavy gun-carriages jolting along their ruts. We follow the course of the advancing Rebels as they press back our troops through the village. Some of our treasured legends meet rough usage at the village hands. John Burns, the veteran hero, turns into a grouty old man, who went out with his gun more to spite his wife than to save his country, — and "Sweet Jenny Wade" is a rank Secessionist, who got no more than her deserts. I only tell such tales as were told to me, vouching for nothing. Not far away is the big rock where General Meade established his head-quarters when driven from the cottage by the roadside. Culp's

Hill we climb on our own feet, and wander among the trees, behind the rough, rambling breastwork of stones and poles. The grove on the hillside is torn by shot and shell beyond even Nature's recuperative power, and it stands stiff and stark, — a dead grove, — a leafless, phantom wood, — strange, sad monument of the terrible conflict. Beyond is Little Round Top, rough and straggling, and heaped with rocks, in whose crevices may lie for years, for aught we know, the bones of those who fell fighting in the good cause, — for the rocks hold their secret well. From its summit we look down into the valley where the slaughter was so great that they call it still the Valley of Death. Here we have another illustration of the disadvantage under which the enemy labored, in never being able to command a view of his whole battle-field. Supposing the woods below to extend nearly to the foot of the hill, he ordered an advance. But between woods and hill is this valley, treacherous with meadow-land, and traversed by a little brook, which still further impeded the progress of his troops. On this low land the exposed soldiers were but a mark for our fire, and the slaughter was fearful. Most interesting of all is Cemetery Hill, so fortunately possessed by our men, so impetuously sought by the foe. Yet marks of the conflict are surprisingly few. A torn paling here and there is seen, but only a single stone in the grave-yard is broken, and that is one erected in memory of a soldier killed at Fair Oaks. The National Cemetery is joined to the village burying-ground, and here the States far and near have gathered their dead, and laid them to rest on the field of their fame. There is another memory here, scarcely less sacred than theirs, — the memory of the beloved President, the nation's last and costliest sacrifice. Here, where the struggle culminated, where the victory was won, though all unknown to victor and vanquished, here the President proclaimed its righteous object, — "That this nation, under God, shall have a new birth of freedom, and that government of the people, by the people, and for the people shall not perish from the earth."

The little country inn is something delightful in these days of big hotels. The landlord is a pleasant-faced, quiet, benevolent old gentleman, who wins your confidence at once. The landlady is active, but not bustling, easy, shrewd, and self-possessed. They have reason to remember the invasion of Pennsylvania, for their own house was one of the first invaded. "They rushed in," she says, "asking, 'Where is Mr. Smith?'"

"'What do you want of Mr. Smith?' says I.

"'We want to take him to Richmond with us.'

"'Indeed,' says I, 'it 's after this I 'm thinking Mr. Smith will go to Richmond with a dirty, greasy Rebel! I 'd think it a *disgrace!*'"

"How did they look?" we ask.

"O, the dirtiest, filthiest, raggedest set you ever saw in your life."

"How did they know anything about Mr. Smith?"

"Some of the citizens, Copperheads, told them. He was a Union man, and known."

"Was he in the house when they were here?"

"Yes, he was stowed away safe enough. But they kept coming. They said they had been told General Meade had his head-quarters here. 'No,' says I, 'he 's got no head-quarters here.

He has no time to stay long anywhere. He is just up to taking care of you.' O, I was just as saucy all day, but I was mute enough at night. They were in and out all night. I had my window open, and I heard one of the officers say, 'Boys, go into that front door and take all you can find.' I went down stairs with a candle in a hurry. They had come into the cellar door, and the room was full of them, and the passage-way.

"'What do you want, gentlemen?' says I.

"'We want to go over the house, to see if there is any Union soldiers secreted here.'

"'No,' says I, 'there 's no Union soldiers in the house, and you can't go over it.'

"'We 'll go up stairs and take a look,' says one of them.

"'No, you can't go up stairs,' says I, 'for I won't let you!'

"Then I heard one of them behind say, 'Boys, let 's go, and leave the lady be.'

"'Yes,' says I, 'that 's just what I want you to do.'

"They hesitated, and I says to the one that spoke, 'Come, you go on, and the rest will follow.' So they just paddled down the cellar stairs again, and I after them with the candle. They never spoke a saucy word to me, — not one, the whole time. They would do anything for a woman. If Mr. Smith had been here we should have fared hard. Only there was one of them who was drunk. He turned round as he was going out and shook his finger under my nose. He was so near he almost touched it. 'Did n't we whip you well to-day?' says he.

"'I don't know,' says I, 'we have n't heard from our men. Perhaps they will tell a different story.'

"'O,' says he, 'we whipped you well, and we 'll whip you worse to-morrow, and Saturday 'll be the worst Fourth of July you ever spent in your life!' But he was drunk.

"Later in the night another regiment came in. They went into the cellar to find the liquor. I told them the liquor was all gone, and I was glad of it. They thought they would just take a look. 'Take as many looks as you like,' says I, 'you 'll find no liquor.' They found all the fish, and carried that out and ate it. They destroyed pretty much everything there was in the basement. That was all the mischief they did. I told them, says I, 'You 've been tormenting me ever since you 've been in town. Now don't stay round all night. Leave the house quiet, so I can get a little rest.' "

"Did they plunder the village much?"

"Yes, they took clothes, furniture, glass, furs, parasols, everything they could lay their hands on. There was no reason in them. Things they did n't want and could n't do anything with. It was the comicalest sight. I saw a man going along that hot day with a great fur tippet round his neck. They 'd wear the things and carry them till they were tired, and then just throw them away. Nice China dishes, and all sorts of things, you could find out in the fields, and under the walls, where they had dropped them."

"Was there any actual fighting near you?"

"O yes! 't was terrible. The cannon kept roaring all day long, and day after day. O, it was so delightful to wake up Saturday and not hear it, — and minute after minute it did not begin. It was just like one peal of heavy thunder all day. There was nine dead bodies right out here on our sidewalk. They could not do anything with them. They just picked them up out of the street and laid them on the sidewalk, and there they had to stay till the battle was over, and our people carried them away. And such warm weather. O, it was dreadful! And they died in such full health. There were eight thousand killed those three days, and not one buried till the fighting was over. And it takes some time then to bury eight thousand men. As much as three miles out, it was horrible. There was one gentleman away from home at the time. His farm was within the line of battle. He could n't get back for ten days after the battle, and then he could n't step foot on his farm only one little corner of it. The dead were buried in his garden and anywhere. A good many people went into their cellars to get away from the shells. There was one family just baking, — they had got their bread into the oven, and they hated to leave it; but the soldiers told them to go down cellar and they would see to the bread. So when the bread was done they had it down there, and the soldiers would rush down and get a piece of bread and butter, and rush back again."

"How did you first hear that the Rebels were defeated?"

"It was in the night. I heard this noise, and I put my head out of the window, and there was the street just full of men. The officers were riding up and down, but there was n't a word said, only tramp, tramp, tramp, all the time. I waked up Mr. Smith, and says I, 'Behold, for the men,' and as soon as he saw it, he said, to be sure, it was a retreat. We could n't hardly believe it. They were so sure. One of the houses where the family had stayed in the midst of the battle, the General came in and got ready to leave. 'Good by, ladies,' says he, 'you 're what we call plucky.'"

"You must have had a good deal of work on your hands after the battle."

"O yes! there was everything to be done, but there was everybody to do it. Everything was done for the wounded that could be done. Doctors and nurses came in from all parts of the country. The Rebels were taken care of just as well as our men. They told about the Gettysburg people not doing anything, but it is not true. They did all they could do."

From Gettysburg the distances begin to shorten, the houses cluster into villages, the villages crystallize into cities, and we are back once more in New England, — rock-bound, frost-bound New England, home of the East Wind, of small-fisted farmers, and strong-minded women, and the Mutual Admiration Society, and the countless brood of heterodoxies in religion and politics, but — New England!

About the sheep-money, do you care to know? In truth I had little to count in solid coin, for all my wool-gathering; but I brought home a Golden Fleece.

And yet, O Reader, gentle but just, if you should whisper that there is great cry and little wool, — alas! I cannot gainsay you.

THE END.

Cambridge: Stereotyped and Printed by Welch, Bigelow, & Co.

www.ingramcontent.com/pod-product-compliance
Lightning Source LLC
LaVergne TN
LVHW020216110826
845151LV00003B/740

* 9 7 8 1 4 2 5 5 3 4 1 7 2 *